A
DEPLORABLE
2018 Election Guide

Steve Stranghoener

For *Ed Norton* and Donald J. Trump: two noteworthy New Yorkers who did their best to drain the swamp in their own special ways.

FOREWORD

Before writing this book, I did what any good writer would do; I tried to define my target market. I had to ask what I meant by Deplorables. This turned out to be a worthwhile endeavor because this election guide proved to be much more inclusive than the title might have indicated. Deplorables were not limited to gun-toting, Bible-believing conservatives like me. Far from it, I found that Deplorables included so called moderates and independents that paid attention to results over rhetoric. Even liberals could be Deplorables, that is, old school liberals that still respected the policies of Democrats like John F. Kennedy. Yes, the Deplorable community had plenty of room for Democrats who believed in giving America's forgotten men, women and minorities a fair shot; a hand up instead of a hand out. Deplorables included everyone that still believed in limited government of, by and for the people.

Almost everyone fit under the big tent except for prisoners locked in ideological dungeons outside of my reach: Hollywood elites, political elites, swamp dwellers (Dem and GOP), anarchists, the mainstream media and woefully dependent wards of the state. The only hope for these poor souls was a miracle cure for the mental illness known as Trump Derangement Syndrome (TDS).

Part One:
Introduction

"We're going to win so much; you're going to be so sick and tired of winning." (Candidate Donald J. Trump)

When I wrote *530 Reasons Why Deplorables Won*, I viewed the 2016 election in the rear view mirror. In an effort to remain as objective as possible, I listed each reason as a single phrase without any analysis or commentary. Not only did I feel the reasons would be self-explanatory but I left it to each reader to form their own opinions. For example, the first seventeen reasons involved Barack Obama and things he'd said or policies he'd implemented. On the surface, I left little room for argument since I didn't embellish the plain facts with my personal slant. Quotes were quotes. Depending on the reader's point of view; liberal, conservative or Deplorable, my citations could have been interpreted differently but all reasonable people had to agree that each reason, whether pro or con, had an impact on how people voted.

This time the elections were on the horizon ahead and so I took a distinctly different approach. By opining at length on each entry, I cast neutrality to the wind and placed my personal views on full display. My earlier Deplorable work, something of a novelty, represented more of an open indictment that left the verdict up to the jury. This time, I prosecuted my case to the best of my ability in order to sway the jurors before they cast their ballots in the 2018 mid-term elections. No, I wasn't impartial in these proceedings and haven't insulted your intelligence by pretending otherwise. I proudly revealed myself as a basket-dwelling Deplorable clinging to my guns and religion. As a patriot, I showed respect for our flag, love for our country, warts and all, stood proudly for our anthem and openly cheered on the President's efforts to drain the swamp and make America great again.

I could have written this book in a more reserved style but then that would have been boring, shallow and disingenuous. In the era of Trump, I felt it only appropriate to pen this tome in Trumpian fashion with guns figuratively blazing in a way that would leave no doubt about my perspective. Accordingly, I've spoken plainly and taken literary license by including plenty of irony and sarcasm. I knew this could cause some to cheer and others to loathe but hoped that, even for the latter, it might garner some appreciation for the humor intended. But make no mistake, attempts at comedy aside, I've taken no prisoners. My observations and criticisms were sometimes blunt, harsh and unyielding. However, I offered no apologies since oftentimes the truth hurt. You could blame it on our Commander in Chief. He rubbed off on me and many others with his refreshing, no-holds-barred approach to leadership.

You might discount some of the entries that follow as insignificant and others as distasteful. Nevertheless, taken as a whole, the case is compelling. Please weigh what I've chronicled carefully. With our 24/7 news cycle, it's almost impossible to keep track of what transpires in a month, much less in a year's time. If nothing else, I hope I've served you by capturing President Trump's first year in office with many helpful reminders. One thing is certain. Whether far-left stalwarts like Nancy Pelosi, Chuck Schumer and Elizabeth Warren or right wingers like Ted Cruz, Jim Jordan and Louie Gohmert or Never-Trump RINOs like Jeff Flake, everyone could agree. President Trump's first year in office was a wild ride unlike any other in history.

Part Two: Honeymoon from Hell

"I want to believe the path you threw out for consideration in Andy's office — that there's no way he gets elected — but I'm afraid we can't take that risk. It's like an insurance policy in the unlikely event you die before you're 40." (FBI Investigator Peter Strzok to his fellow FBI Agent and mistress, Lisa Page)

After a presidential election, the losing candidate typically offered a noble concession before fading into the background to lick his wounds. Even in the hotly contested 2000 election that required a recount involving hanging chad in Florida, Al Gore conceded to George W. Bush respectfully for the good of the country in a manner befitting a statesman. He left the political limelight and started his crusade against global warming. Although this hoax amounted to nothing more than a money and power grab we forgave the lunacy this fomented among enviromaniacs. Deplorables even suppressed the urge to guffaw at God's lampooning sense of humor in somehow causing arctic conditions to follow Mr. Gore on his pied piper journeys around the world. We gave credit where credit was due to the former Vice President for showing proper decorum in accepting the reality of W's razor thin victory.

If only Donald Trump were so lucky! Alas, Hillary Clinton never really accepted defeat. She drug her feet when it came time to concede. This seemed unsightly and hypocritical for someone who had badgered Donald Trump on the campaign trail for not unequivocally declaring he would concede after losing. Even after offering a half-hearted concession, Mrs. Clinton didn't waste time in mounting an excuse extravaganza of epic proportions ... that is, after she came out of her long walk in the woods. She swore that she accepted full responsibility for her monumental loss but, in the next breath, spewed rationalizations ad nauseam and furiously pointed fingers in every outward direction.

At first she and the media labored over the fact she'd won the popular vote and went so far as to call for the elimination of the Electoral College. This actually proved to be a worthwhile exercise in that it initiated a debate that shed light on a heretofore largely misunderstood part of our process under a democratic republic. People learned about the importance of states' rights. It revealed that the spread in the popular vote could be tied to a single, populous blue state, California, where Donald Trump didn't campaign much.

Dissecting the data just highlighted that Trump had won by a landslide and reinforced the wisdom of the Founders in establishing the Electoral College and fine tuning it through the Twelfth Amendment to the Constitution. Donald Trump won thirty states to Hillary Clinton's twenty-one including the District of Columbia. He bested her three-hundred-six (somehow later adjusted to three-hundred-four) to two-hundred-thirty-two in the Electoral College and garnered wins in twenty-six-hundred of the nation's thirty-one-hundred counties for a whopping eighty-four percent of the U. S's total geography.

Thereafter, Hillary became a darling of the talk shows and popped up here, there and everywhere to offer a breath-taking list of excuses. First there was Jim Comey. Then she claimed another right-wing conspiracy fueled by Trump's racist followers. Yes, she did it again and labeled all of us who supported Donald Trump as Deplorables ... racists, misogynists and homophobic, ignorant hillbillies. She went on and on, much to the delight of the media who had cried hysterically on election night. Every now and then she paused momentarily to assure us she took full responsibility. However, she never stared truth in the face to admit she'd been a lousy candidate who offered nothing more than four more years of Obamanomics while taking states like Wisconsin and Michigan for granted. Her campaign strategy counted on only two factors: the gender card and anti-Trump rhetoric.

As people tired of her and even a few on the Left longed for her to go away, she started singing a different tune called Russia, Russia; Russia. This seemed to resonate as the chorus echoed from every direction. This offered a welcome diversion to the media who simply couldn't accept the reality of a Trump presidency. Normally, a new administration was allowed a grace period of two months to get their ducks in a row before the inauguration. During this transition period, the Washington Press Corps typically adopted a wait-and-see posture while the incoming administration attempted to find its sea legs. This time around, they bounced conventional wisdom out on its ear.

Sour grapes fermented into an intoxicating mixture that fueled a strange form of blind resistance. The media acted as if Donald Trump had somehow stolen the election from the Anointed One, Her Highness Queen Hillary. Democrats, the media and shell-shocked Hillary supporters coalesced into an impervious opposition that had two things in common: their hatred of Donald Trump and inability to accept the election results. This resistance movement became a cause celebre that manifested itself in every way possible from social media to entertainment and, most prominently, mainstream news outlets. Instead of a grace period, the Trump transition team faced what amounted to an all-out declaration of war.

Transitions were usually followed by a honeymoon period where a new administration was given one-hundred days to cast off and chart a course while laying down a few prominent markers pointing to the way ahead. Even most conservative administrations were given some benefit of the doubt. In this case, no quarter was given in an onslaught that started as a firefight from day one. The media couldn't even afford one *Kumbaya* moment from the inauguration but instead initiated a huge, meaningless controversy over the magnitude of the gathering. They tried to downplay the size of the inauguration crowd as if it amounted to a rejection of the Trump Administration from the American people. President Trump responded in typical fashion and perpetuated a war with the media that had benefitted him immensely during the 2016 campaign.

The media refused to offer a modicum of respect for the President or even the office as long as Donald

Trump occupied it. They unleashed an avalanche of bad press unprecedented in American history even during the Watergate days of Richard Nixon's presidency. Independent studies revealed that stories related to Donald Trump during the first one-hundred days of his presidency were negative eighty-nine percent of the time. This number included Fox News! Without FNC, the coverage was virtually one-hundred percent negative. They parsed every word and put the worst construction on everything the President and his team said or did. When that wasn't enough, they made up stories prompting President Trump to further popularize the fake news label he'd applied so effectively during the campaign.

The flood of venom directed at the President wasn't limited to liberals or Democrats. Many establishment Republicans, RINOs and Never-Trumpers jumped on the band wagon. Everyone outside his Deplorable base appeared to be intent on derailing the Trump Train before it left the station. Surely Donald Trump must have wondered why he ran for president and perhaps even rued the day he'd won. However, he gave no evidence of harboring such doubts. Still, supporters including faithful Deplorables worried that, now in office and facing such furious opposition, President Trump would rush to the center like so many before him and start appeasing the opposition with one compromise after another. Amazingly, he laid out an agenda that mirrored the platform upon which he'd been elected. No, he didn't back down but instead remained the furious counter-puncher who fought fire with fire.

This only served to infuriate the opposition which dug in its heels further. Time and again they criticized Donald Trump for not being presidential. Dems and Republicans alike scolded his continued use of social media to get the truth out in his unadulterated fashion. Deplorables gleefully shouted *hell yeah* with each outrageously truthful tweet and marveled in thankfulness that President Trump refused to be presidential. By presidential, his critics meant for him to be a timid, double-talking, politically correct mouthpiece for the D. C. establishment. President Trump completely defied convention and regularly riled the Washington elites with his common sense and plain talk.

Yes, Donald Trump remained a true outsider; a rebel who intended to follow through on his promise to drain the swamp in our nation's capital. This galvanized establishment Democrats and Republicans who wanted to maintain the status quo at all costs. This unholy alliance of Washington, New York and Hollywood power brokers congealed into a toxic mixture of entrenched elites … soon to become known as the Deep State … fixated on bringing down Donald Trump. It seemed the true outsider who had hitched his wagon to the tenuous fortunes of America's forgotten men and women had his back to a precipitous cliff. His unique brand of conservative populism appeared doomed from the start. His transition period and first one-hundred days in office amounted to nothing short of a honeymoon from hell.

Part Three: Swamp Fever

"This executive order was mean spirited and un-American." (Senate Minority Leader, "Crying" Chuck Schumer, referring to President Trump's travel ban on January 30, 2017)

"This is Armageddon." (House Minority Leader, Nancy "Chicken Little" Pelosi, referring to the GOP tax cut bill on December 4, 2017)

In this section, I've included a chronology of selected events representative of the news reported during President Trump's opening year in office through his first State of the Union Address. Each entry is listed by the date when the events occurred or were reported by media outlets. With so many negative entries, you might wonder why I didn't commit more space to the incredible, sometimes historic accomplishments achieved during the President's inaugural year. Simply put, I've just relayed matters the way the media so often portrayed them. Not to worry, I've counter-balanced the media's pronounced bias with plenty of facts and editorial remarks to shed light on the truth that so often eluded or was intentionally omitted by poison-penned reporters.

Entries earlier in the year have tended to be brief and accompanied by less commentary. That's because I wanted you to experience these reports as they occurred in real time. As we moved throughout the year and patterns emerged, my remarks became more pointed and interconnected. From hindsight, I could have revised the earlier entries to fit what later became obvious patterns. However, it seemed to be a worthy exercise to allow readers to discover these trends as they bubbled up naturally throughout the chronology.

This exercise should undoubtedly bring back memories that will raise your ire. Taken individually, they might boost your Deplorable blood pressure a bit but I must caution you. If you read through this collective list in one sitting, it could cause your blood to boil at the unprecedented indecency and injustice inflicted upon the President. Extreme, irrational bias fueled by bitter hatred of President Trump and his Deplorable supporters descended into delusional lunacy that could only be explained as a form of mental illness known as Trump Derangement Syndrome (TDS). A Machiavellian outlook encompassed the opposition in a grip so tight it led to outright lying as an acceptable journalistic means by which to conduct their search-and-destroy missions.

Despite the strong temptation to fight fire with fire, I implore you to lay aside your Deplorable emotions and concentrate on the real danger here. The opposition or so-called resistance wants to do more than just undermine the Trump presidency. If they have their way, we will cease to exist as a constitutional republic of, by and for the people. Yes, if you follow the thread laid down by liberals and their media enablers, you will see the truth that this is all about the will of a free and independent people being pitted against liberal elites who worship government rather than God.

2/2/17: Rioters at the University of California at Berkeley employed violence to force the cancellation of a speech by Milo Yiannopoulos; a gay man ... usually a cause celebre of the Left ... who also happened to be a conservative libertarian. The mainstream media gleefully reported this as some kind of civil rights triumph rather than a gross violation of our First Amendment rights.

2/17/17: "Dreamer" Juan Manuel Montes (twenty-three) was deported after forfeiting his DACA status by leaving the U. S. surreptitiously in violation of DACA rules and trying to cross the border illegally again. The mainstream media used the case to criticize the Trump Administration and Montes hired an attorney to sue the Department of Homeland Security (DHS).

2/26/17: Newly elected DNC Party Chairman Tom Perez launched his tenure with an expletive-laced tirade against President Trump. He set the tone for the Dem's resistance platform as being against everything Trump rather than for anything. The Dems, I supposed, threw a bone to their far-left, Bernie-loving base by electing Minnesota Congressman Keith Ellison as Deputy. As the country's only Muslim House member, he had sometimes appeared more sympathetic to our terrorist enemies than American citizens.

3/1/17: Defying the "experts" like Paul Krugman who predicted a market crash that we'd never recover from, the DOW set a new record at twenty-one-thousand.

3/22/17: President Trump received an avalanche of criticism from the media for claiming earlier that the Obama Administration had wire tapped his campaign. They made the President out to be a liar. Congressman Devin Nunes, the House Intelligence Committee Chairman, confirmed that members of the Trump campaign team had been caught up in surveillance by the Obama Justice Department that was directed at foreign sources. Unwilling to admit that the President had been correct; the media parsed words to say the spying was "inadvertent" and "wire-tapping" was a technically incorrect term. Deplorables shouted *surveillance is surveillance*!

4/6/17: It riled the media that President Trump played it close to the vest in military matters so as to keep our enemies guessing. He didn't draw red lines like President Obama only to ignore them later. Case in point, the President ordered a military strike on Syria with fifty-nine Tomahawk Cruise Missiles hitting the air base from which Syria had launched a chemical weapons attack against their own civilians. The media had a tough time ignoring the swift, decisive move that brought accolades from even some Democrats.

President Trump surprised Chinese President Xi Jinping over dessert during their dinner meeting at his Mar-a-Lago resort in Palm Beach, FL with an up-to-the-minute report on the Cruise Missile strike in Syria. President Xi responded soon thereafter with support for our sanctions by refusing N. Korean coal shipments to China in order to apply economic pressure. President Trump hadn't talked softly but he carried a big stick in exercising diplomacy through strength to reassert American leadership abroad.

4/7/17: The GOP-controlled Senate unleashed the "nuclear option" to stop obstructionist Democrats and confirmed Neil Gorsuch as an Associate Justice on the U. S. Supreme Court by a simple majority vote which included four throw-in Democrat votes in the affirmative.

Due to the no-nonsense attitude of the President, his Attorney General Jeff Sessions and DHS Secretary John Kelly in enforcing existing laws, reports grudgingly trickled out that illegal immigration dropped seventy percent in the Administration's first one-hundred days. The media also tried to ignore the good news that economic indicators of consumer and business confidence soared during the Administration's first one-hundred days. Mostly they tried to put a negative spin on any such successes or ignored them altogether.

4/8/17: Swedish authorities confirmed that a Muslim terrorist was responsible for the truck attack in Stockholm that killed and badly injured multiple victims. During his 2016 election campaign, the media roundly criticized Donald Trump for warning of terrorism in Sweden due to their open border immigration policy. According to the mocking media, such a notion seemed ludicrous in the peace-loving Nordic nation.

4/9/17: We heard nothing but crickets from the mainstream media when forty-four Coptic Christians were slaughtered and over one-hundred others were injured by Muslim terrorists in Egypt during their Palm Sunday church service.

4/14/17: The U. S. Military dropped the "Mother of All Bombs," the largest non-nuclear conventional weapon ever used in combat (twenty-one-thousand pound explosive charge), killing dozens of ISIS fighters in a remote, mountainous region of Eastern Afghanistan along the border near Pakistan. This gave a clear indication of the President's intent to follow through on his pledge to get tough on the terrorists.

The media chided President Trump for claiming that voter fraud occurred in the 2016 election. They said this amounted to a diversion from the real problem: Russian collusion. Kansas Secretary of State Kris Kobach released preliminary results proving that non-U. S. citizens had illegally voted. Deplorables just muttered *I told you so* as time proved President Trump correct once again.

4/15/17: North Korea's Kim Jong-un defied the U. S. and U. N. by test firing another missile but it blew up almost immediately after launch. When asked about rumors that the U. S. had destroyed the missile using cyber warfare, the Administration refused to comment, leaving the North Korean dictator to worry about U. S. capabilities.

4/16/17: U. S. citizen Aya Hijazi was released from detention in Egypt, after nearly three years of President Obama's foot dragging, thanks to President Trump's direct intervention during negotiations with Egyptian President Abdel-Fattah el-Sissi. Not willing to give credit where credit was due, the liberal media mostly ignored President Trump's efforts rather than celebrating it as they should have. Perhaps they didn't want to make President Obama look bad by comparison.

4/17/17: Vice President Mike Pence traveled to the demilitarized zone separating North and South Korea and echoed the U. S.' new stance toward the rogue nation of North Korea and their unstable dictator Kim Jong-un. In keeping with earlier messages from President Trump, Secretary of State Rex Tillerson and Defense Secretary James Mattis, VP Pence said the U. S.' patience with N. Korea had run out.

4/18/17: Various liberal news outlets beat the drums about collusion between Russia and the Trump campaign. Mysterious leaks from inside the Justice Department seemed to add fuel to the fire. President Trump brushed off the Russian hoax as fake news.

Russian TU-95 "Bear" bombers buzzed Alaska about forty miles off the coast in an ongoing effort to antagonize the US through saber rattling. This seemed like an odd way for Vladimir Putin to thank President Trump for supposedly colluding with him.

4/19/17: Black man Kori Ali Muhammed shot and killed three white men in Fresno, CA and the city and mainstream media labeled it a hate crime but wouldn't call it terrorism despite Muhammed shouting "Allahu Akbar" during the rampage.

In what appeared to be a trending liberal witch hunt against conservative commentators, Fox News fired Bill O'Reilly for purported sexual improprieties. In O'Reilly's words, his dismissal was "due to completely unfounded claims." Deplorables wondered how the mainstream media could justify their continued love affair with former President Bill Clinton in such an environment.

Missouri Democrat Congressman William Lacy Clay continued his absurd, months-long campaign to restore a piece of art to the halls of the U. S. Capital Building that depicted police officers as pigs. Deplorables like me in St. Louis were assuaged by the fact that, even though we no longer had the NFL Rams and thus couldn't personally witness the likes of Colin Kaepernick disrespecting our nation, flag, veterans and law enforcement, we at least had Lacy Clay ... NOT!

4/20/17: Yet another ISIS terrorist attack occurred in Paris. Deplorables wondered how there could be gun violence in a country where guns were illegal.

A melee erupted in Berkeley, CA when Trump supporters held a rally in a local park. An anarchistic mob of violent liberals posed as protectors of free speech while actually eschewing the First Amendment rights of conservatives. They employed brutish, fascist tactics while labeling Trump's supporters as fascists.

4/21/17: The Trump Administration announced plans to get tough on illegal immigration by withholding federal funds from sanctuary cities that defied federal immigration laws. Various Sanctuary city mayors led by Chicago's Rahm Emanuel and New York City's Bill DeBlasio fired back defiantly, vowing to resist at all costs.

4/24/17: The U. N. added those renowned women's rights advocates, Saudi Arabia, to their Women's Rights Commission. Deplorables couldn't hear a peep out of Helen Reddy, much less any roaring.

4/25/17: The loony-liberal, activist Ninth Circuit went bananas again and blocked President Trump's executive order requiring that sanctuary cities comply with existing federal immigration law.

The mainstream media described the Muslim practice of punishing women through Female Genital Mutilation (FGM) as merely "cutting" while others cheered when Ivanka Trump was heckled, jeered and booed at a women's conference in Berlin hosted by German Chancellor Angela Merkel.

Iranian provocations continued when a Republican Guard vessel approached within three-thousand feet of a U. S. guided missile destroyer in the Persian Gulf. The USS Mahan was forced to fire warning flares after the Iranians ignored radio contact. Was this the legacy President Obama had left us through his nuclear deal with Tehran?

Democrats howled that President Trump acted unconstitutionally when he threatened to withhold federal funds from sanctuary cities that refused to uphold existing federal immigration laws passed by Congress. Deplorables recalled how these same hypocrites applauded President Obama when he had threatened to withhold federal funds from cities that violated no laws when they refused to allow transgender boys into bathrooms used by girls.

4/27/17: Bill Nye the pseudo "Science Guy" proposed population control as a remedy to climate change problems. This echoed Communist China's limits on children and America's 1970s push for Zero Population Growth in response to another "scientific" hoax; that the world could not produce enough food to support the growing population. This previously debunked fallacy originated by Thomas Malthus in 1798 was popularized in America by Stanford Professor Paul Erlich's book, The Population Bomb (1968).

The University of California at Berkeley, self-touted as the well-spring and defender of free speech in the 1960s, again shut down the First Amendment rights of conservatives by barring Ann Coulter from speaking at the invitation of conservative students while citing their supposed inability to provide security.

5/1/17: May Day protests and demonstrations against President Trump and in favor of illegal immigration and open borders supplanted the traditional workers' rights parades.

5/3/17: Hillary Clinton told Christine Amanpour that she accepted responsibility for losing the election and in the next breath blamed FBI Director James Comey and WikiLeaks for her loss. Although six long months had passed since President Trump's landslide election, Deplorables had to wonder if she would ever go away.

5/4/17: Immediately after the House health care bill passed, Democrats began singing a familiar classic … *Na-na, hey-hey, goodbye.* The Dems implied that the Republicans who voted for the bill would lose seats in 2018. Deplorables asked if Democrats would ever learn.

5/6/17: Barack Obama made a public plea for his "friends in France" to vote for Emmanuel Macron for President, demonstrating his preference for globalism over America-first nationalism. This interference in a foreign election was lauded by the media while they ostracized Vladimir Putin for interfering in foreign elections and repeated the hoax that Donald Trump had colluded with Putin. Deplorables remembered when then President Obama had openly tried to influence the Israeli electorate against the re-election of Benjamin Netanyahu.

5/9/17: After complaining for months how they'd lost confidence in FBI Director James Comey and calling for his resignation, Democrats became hysterical when President Trump fired him.

Harvard reintroduced segregation by conducting a separate ceremony for their 2017 black graduates.

5/10/17: Constantino Banda-Acosta seriously injured a six-year-old boy in San Diego while driving drunk. He had been deported fifteen times previously and had committed a long list of crimes. The young boy required multiple surgeries for a skull fracture.

5/14/17: Florida Memorial University posthumously awarded a B. S. Aeronautical Science degree to Trayvon Martin. I sent a note-to-self saying, "don't ever send your kids or grandkids to FMU!"

5/15/17: The Washington Post issued an unsubstantiated story that President Trump shared classified intelligence with Russia during a White House meeting. The mainstream ran with the story despite public testimony from U. S. National Security Advisor H. R. McMaster that the story wasn't true. McMaster was one of only four Americans in the meeting. Secretary of State Rex Tillerson, another attendee, also denied the WAPO story.

While the WAPO spewed fake news, another story broke showing that former DNC Staffer Seth

Rich, not the Russians, had leaked emails to WikiLeaks. Deplorables recalled that Seth Rich had been gunned down for no apparent reason on 7/10/16 at the height of the campaign. The mainstream media largely ignored the story despite the possible cover up. Deplorables couldn't ignore the "coincidence" of yet another person close to the Clinton Machine that had met an untimely death.

5/17/17: The Justice Department appointed a Special Counsel (not Special Prosecutor because there was no evidence of a crime) to lead the investigation into the bogus Russian/Trump collusion claims. Deplorables took this as the latest evidence of GOP spinelessness following AG Jeff Sessions' recusal from the Russian investigation.

Thanks to former President Barack Obama, Bradley/Chelsea Manning was released from prison after seven years of a thirty-five-year sentence for leaking classified information to WikiLeaks. Ironically, his/her release came on the same day that a Special Counsel was assigned to investigate Russia's role in leaking information to WikiLeaks that supposedly lost the 2016 election for Hillary Clinton.

5/20/17: President Trump made an historic visit to Saudi Arabia where he was warmly received by King Salman and dramatically reset our relationship with the Saudis.

5/22/17: On his next stop, President Trump met with Israeli President Rivlin who said Israel was happy to have the United States back. PM Benjamin Netanyahu lauded the President for bringing new hope and energy to the peace process. Rather than reporting on the incredibly positive way these foreign leaders received President Trump, the online liberal news services like Yahoo and AOL pushed a fake story that Melania Trump had slapped away President Trump's hand.

While ignoring opportunities to pursue job growth and security, liberal Democrat mayors in New Orleans, St. Louis and elsewhere tried to re-prosecute the Civil War by demanding the removal of historic statues of Confederate military figures. St. Louis's new Mayor Lyda Krewson also pushed to make St. Louis an abortion sanctuary city. It somehow escaped her attention during her crusades that, during the past weekend, nine more St. Louisans had been shot and four died. In Chicago, the murder capital of the world, Mayor Rahm Emanuel worked to protect illegal immigrants including many who had committed other serious crimes while their murder rate continued to explode.

ISIS terrorists bombed an Ariana Grande concert in Manchester England killing twenty-two and injuring fifty-nine at the time of this writing including young girls and children. CNN largely ignored reporting on the tragedy in order to continue their insane assaults on President Trump thus choosing ideological ranting over news reporting. Deplorables noted that this horrific mass murder occurred in Great Britain despite their total ban on guns.

5/23/17: After the tragedy at her concert in Manchester England, Ariana Grande scurried back to the United States, the country that she criticized so vehemently after President Trump's election. Of course she was protected by armed security.

Another air-headed pop icon, Katy Perry, opined after Manchester that we needed to respond to the tragedy by coming together with open borders to coexist.

5/24/17: Always looking to put the worst construction on everything Trump, the mainstream media summed up President Trump's visit to the Vatican by complaining that Melania and Ivanka wore veils in their meeting with the Pope but refused to wear head scarfs in Saudi Arabia.

President Trump's visit with the Pope started on a cautious note since both men had made negative statements toward the other in the past. The Pope had a sullen look on his face during their first photo op. After meeting personally for the first time, they both smiled and offered an optimistic outlook based on common ground. The mainstream media used the first photo to throw cold water on the entire meeting.

5/25/17: The media blamed Donald Trump when Montana congressional special election candidate Greg Gianforte body slamming overzealous Guardian reporter Ben Jacobs while the President was five-thousand miles away in Belgium. Deplorables smiled when Gianforte still won the election on that very same night.

5/29/17: The mainstream media didn't seem to notice when the Pope displayed the same dour face as he had with President Trump when he first met with Canadian Prime Minister Justin Trudeau. Research revealed that the Pope had displayed the same countenance when meeting other world leaders including Barack Obama. Yet they continued to drive the narrative that the Pope disliked President Trump.

5/30/17: Hundreds of illegal aliens swarmed the Texas State House to protest the new state law that required law enforcement and local governments to follow federal immigration laws. Ironically, the protesters openly flaunted their illegal status which prompted one Republican lawmaker to contact ICE. This resulted in a near brawl between Democrats and Republicans. Incredibly, Democrats were incensed that someone contacted law enforcement to stop disruptive, threatening protesters who openly admitted to breaking federal immigration laws that the new Texas law was designed to enforce.

5/31/17: Democrats on the House Intelligence Committee who had called for Carter Page to testify in the never ending Russian collusion investigation did an about face and said they no longer wanted his testimony. This came amid reports that Page wanted to testify to clear up false rumors circulated about him and purportedly had evidence to prove that former FBI Director James Comey and Former CIA Director John Brennan lied during their testimony to the Committee.

Fading comedienne Kathy Griffin offered a pathetic non-apology apology for posing with a bloody severed head of a Donald Trump likeness. While some in the mainstream media denounced her atrocious act, she largely received a pass. CNN grudgingly fired Griffin from her New Year's Eve gig when people pointed out how CNN had led the charge in getting a rodeo clown banned for life for wearing an Obama mask.

6/1/17: Still unable to accept responsibility for her election loss eight months prior, Hillary Clinton doubled down and called the majority of Americans deplorable again! She claimed that Donald Trump won because he was very good at tapping into peoples' misogyny, homophobia, xenophobia, Islamophobia, etc.

6/2/17: Two days after issuing her non-apology apology, Kathy Griffin held a bizarre news conference with an attorney present and claimed to be the victim. She accused President Trump of being a bully and said behind crocodile tears, "He broke me." Apparently, she forgot that she ruined her own career by posing in ISIS-like fashion while holding up a blood soaked, severed Trump head.

6/3/17: We suffered through yet another terrorist attack in Great Britain where ISIS-backed savages in a van ran down pedestrians on London Bridge and then marauded through several bars slashing peoples' throats initially leaving seven dead and forty-eight wounded. London's Muslim Mayor Sadiq Khan said there was "no reason to be alarmed" and claimed "London is one of the safest global cities in the world." After President Trump criticized Khan, U. S. Ambassador Lewis Lukens, an Obama holdover, supported Khan and offered him praise. Deplorables again noted that a horrific mass murder had been perpetrated in Great Britain where guns had been totally banned.

6/5/17: ISIS claimed responsibility for a terrorist attack in Melbourne, Australia where the gunman killed one man and held a woman hostage. How did the terrorist get a gun since they'd been banned in Australia?

6/6/17: Amidst what seemed to be daily terror attacks during the so called holy month of Ramadan, a man claiming allegiance to ISIS attacked a French police officer with a hammer outside of Notre Dame Cathedral while yelling, "This is for Syria." Deplorables called for hammers to be banned … NOT!

6/7/17: The NYT reportedly exposed CIA Operative Michael D'Andrea, put his life at risk and jeopardized various counter-intelligence efforts. This news reinforced President Trump's claim that the mainstream media was the enemy of the American people.

6/8/17: James Comey testified before the Senate Intelligence Committee and revealed that, during the investigation into Hillary Clinton's use of a private email server for government business, Attorney General Loretta Lynch instructed him to refer to the situation as a "matter" rather than an investigation. Comey admitted to going along with this even though he knew it was wrong. This apparent obstruction of justice to protect Hillary's presidential ambitions followed shortly after Loretta Lynch met with Bill Clinton on a private jet despite the ongoing investigation of Hillary. Yet, the liberal media didn't trumpet this significant news but rather reported that Comey could not trust President Trump to tell the truth.

Comey confirmed that he had told Donald Trump he wasn't personally under investigation and said that President Trump's request for loyalty hadn't constituted obstruction of justice. After seven months, still no evidence had been produced to support the claim that the Trump campaign colluded with Russia. Also, even though evidence showed that the Russians supposedly tried to hack into our election system, one-hundred percent of the testimony supported that Russia had not in any way influenced the outcome of the election. Yet, the Democrats and their pals in the media continued to push the Russian collusion narrative while obstructing every effort of the Trump

Administration to implement the agenda that reflected the will of the voters.

6/10/17: The tax payer supported New York Public Theater staged a production of *Julius Caesar* during their summertime Free Shakespeare in the Park promotion. They depicted the Roman ruler as a Donald Trump clone replete with a dark suit, long red tie and bushy blond hair. The play climaxed with the Trump lookalike being stabbed to death by a mob of his angry peers.

6/14/17: James Hodgkinson of Belleville, IL opened fire on congressmen practicing in Alexandria, VA for a charity baseball game. He shot and injured five people including Steve Scalise, the Majority Whip in the House of Representatives. Hodgkinson, who was killed by Capitol Police from Scalise's security detail, was an outspoken supporter of Bernie Sanders and avowed member of the resistance movement against President Trump.

Prior to the shooting, Hodgkinson asked several people if the ballplayers were on the Republican or Democrat team. Although Hodgkinson was apparently mentally unbalanced, a strong argument could have been made that he was incited by the extreme vitriol of malcontents like Kathy Griffin who posed with the mock, bloody head of President Trump and the New York theater group who staged a version of *Julius Caesar* depicting his bloody assassination using a Donald Trump lookalike as the victim.

6/19/17: Affinity Magazine blamed Otto Warmbier's death on Warmbier and his "white privilege." They ignored the fact that Kim Jong-un and his repressive regime murdered Warmbier for stealing a poster and scolded the dead young American saying he should have respected North Korea's laws. Affinity on the other hand didn't think illegal immigrants needed to respect U. S. immigration laws.

6/20/17: Members of the mainstream media blamed Rep. Steve Scalise for getting shot by a politically motivated left-wing fanatic who possessed a hit list of conservative Republicans. The media said Scalise brought this on himself through his conservative rhetoric and open support of the Second Amendment.

6/22/17: The Left continued to incite violence when actor Johnny Depp harkened back to the last time an actor assassinated a President, referring to how John Wilkes Booth had shot Abraham Lincoln, and stated that it was time for it to happen again.

Nebraska Democrat Party Official Phil Montag was forced to resign after saying he wished Steve Scalise had died.

7/2/17: Former President Barack Obama pulled a decorum-and-tradition-destroying trifecta by publicly criticizing his successor, President Trump, during our nation's Independence Day holiday weekend in a foreign country; namely Muslim-majority Philippines.

7/4/17: MSNBC celebrated our nation's independence by allowing political analyst Joan Walsh to opine that Donald Trump won the 2016 presidential election because Trump voters feared brown people. Deplorables wondered how long the Dems could continue to read from the same, tired script: denial, identity politics and the old reliable race card. In effect, Joan Walsh repeated what got Hillary Clinton into hot water by claiming that half of Americans were deplorable.

America continued to pay the price for former President Obama's absurd, do-nothing foreign policy he had labeled as strategic patience (pure sophistry like his famous claim of leading from behind). North Korea tested an ICBM that demonstrated the ability to potentially deliver a nuclear warhead to Alaska.

7/5/17: Oregon passed a state law requiring insurers to cover the cost of abortions. Oregon joined California as the second state to require insurers to pay the cost of murdering babies. This reinforced the Democratic Party's reputation as anti-God.

A black NYC policewoman, Miosotis Familia, was assassinated while sitting in her patrol car. The forty-eight-year-old mother of three was gunned down by Alexander Bonds without warning. NYC Mayor Bill De Blasio didn't attend the vigil for the slain officer.

7/6/17: MSNBC produced more fake news; this time from the G20 Summit in Hamburg, Germany. They showed a clip of the Polish First Lady walking past President Trump to shake hands with Melania Trump and claimed she snubbed the President. They cut the clip short to hide the fact that seconds later the Polish First Lady greeted President Trump warmly and shook his hand.

7/7/17: Mentally ill, liberal Mayor Bill De Blasio skipped the swearing in ceremony of over five-hundred new NYPD officers to catch a flight to Hamburg to join in the G20 protests against capitalism. He served as the keynote speaker for the "Hamburg Shows Attitude" demonstration. When questioned about shirking his duties as Mayor to support violent protesters in Hamburg, De Blasio said he felt committed to show resistance against Donald Trump.

7/8/17: The mainstream media went berserk when President Trump asked Ivanka to hold his seat at the table at the G20 Conference while he attended to other business for a short time. They launched into the Dems' all-too-familiar war on conservative women, screamed nepotism and claimed Ivanka was unqualified even though the topic had shifted to one of Ivanka's strengths: promoting female entrepreneurship in Africa. Angela Merkel came to Ivanka's defense since there was plenty of precedence for U. S. and other leaders doing so. Still the media latched onto this nonsense rather than talking about President Trump's many successes at the G20.

7/10/17: Fox News reported that James Comey's memos that he admitted leaking to the NYT contained classified information; a crime. The mainstream media ignored the story. Instead they tried to resuscitate the Russian collusion hoax by reporting on a meeting between Donald Trump, Jr. and a Russian woman promoting the adoption of Russian children.

The University of Missouri faced a thirty-five percent drop in freshman enrollment, budget reductions and staff cuts as fallout from their foolish support of Black Lives Matter (BLM) and Ferguson-related protesters on campus in 2015. Unwilling or unable to accept the truth, they blamed the damaging results on racism. In order to remedy the situation in their minds, the liberal loons in charge of the University decided to require diversity training for all incoming freshmen, a move that exacerbated the drop in enrollment.

7/11/17: President Trump sent a tweet expressing his displeasure over Chuck Schumer and his Democrat colleagues' obstructionism citing this evidence: almost six months after taking office, only forty-eight of his one-hundred-ninety-eight nominees had been confirmed by the Senate.

The Associated Press demonstrated their extreme liberal bias by publishing their latest style book that included restrictions against using the following words deemed too conservative: Islamist, migrant, refugee and pro-life. The new guidelines said news stories should reference "militants" in place of terms like Islamists and terrorists.

7/16/17: Canadian Prime Minister Justin Trudeau announced that the Canadian Government would apologize to Omar Khadr and award him $10 million for his troubles. Apparently, the Canadian government, outside of a court of law, decided it had wronged Canadian citizen Khadr by arresting him for crimes committed as a fifteen-year-old terrorist in Afghanistan where he murdered one American soldier and blinded another. Did Trudeau do this to thumb his nose at America and President Trump? The widow of the dead soldier received nothing. According to news sources, many Canadians were enraged by Trudeau's actions. Deplorables wondered why he would waste political capital without the solid backing of the Canadian people. This served as another sign that liberalism had become a mental illness.

7/17/17: Incredibly, forty-six mentally ill Republicans joined with Democrats to defeat an amendment to the defense spending bill that would have stripped out billions of dollars to be wasted by the DOD to study climate change. Instead of spending these hard earned tax dollars on strengthening the military, they aimed to squander this money on perpetuating the false religion and grand hoax of climate change. Sane people wondered how this ever became a priority for our military.

Good news ... the Congress gave President Trump $36 billion more than he requested for defense spending. Bad news … in addition to studying climate change, the extra money was allotted to promote the mental illness of transgenderism. The DOD planned to spend the money on sex changes and hormone treatments. Sane people wondered how this made our military stronger.

7/18/17: Senators Shelley Moore Capito of West Virginia, Lisa Murkowski of Alaska and Susan Collins of Maine announced they would not support a straight repeal of Obamacare after the latest GOP Senate bill to repeal and replace Obamacare failed. Only eighteen months earlier they had voted yes for this measure when it didn't count because of President Obama's veto power.

7/19/17: The mainstream media continued its fake news assault on President Trump by heralding sensational headlines claiming that the President had a second, secret meeting with Vladimir Putin at the G20 Summit in Germany. As it turned out, the "secret meeting" was a dinner hosted by Angela Merkel that was attended by the twenty world leaders and their spouses along with dozens of media and photographers. Melania Trump was assigned a seat next to Putin while President Trump was seated separately, nowhere near Putin. There was no meeting and no secrecy … just more fake news.

7/21/17: The liberal media put their hypocritical double standard on display by launching personal attacks against Sarah Huckabee Sanders including demeaning comments about her appearance. Shortly after she was promoted to White House Spokeswoman, only the third woman to hold this post, the media attacked her on the basis of her gender demonstrating that their so called support for feminism only extended to liberal women.

7/23/17: At least nine people died when a trucker smuggled a trailer crammed with illegal immigrants into Texas in one-hundred degree heat. Some in the conservative media rightly noted that these deaths could be attributed to the lure of sanctuary cities that prompted these folks to take such risks.

At the same time that illegal immigrants were dying of heat exposure in the back of a tractor trailer in Texas, Massachusetts passed a law requiring police to ignore federal immigration law and not cooperate with ICE. Deplorables were stunned ... a sanctuary state codified a law to undermine the rule of law!

7/24/17: Sen. Minority Leader Chuck Schumer announced at a press conference that the Democrats were to blame for their election losses in 2010, 2012 and 2016 for not offering a cogent message other than being anti-Trump in 2016. But he didn't call for an end to the ridiculous, politically motivated farce known as the Russian collusion investigation.

7/25/17: GOP Senators Lisa Murkowski and Susan Collins of Maine voted no on whether to allow debate on the repeal and replacement of Obamacare. Deplorables tried to fathom the irony of two GOP Senators refusing to even debate the question after seven years of GOP promises to repeal Obamacare. Senator Murkowski had even voted to repeal it earlier when she knew she'd be protected by President Obama's veto power. Thankfully, the measure passed by the slimmest of margins with Vice President Pence breaking the fifty-fifty deadlock.

President Trump defiantly continued to tweet his displeasure over the Russian hoax by stating that the investigative committees would probably go after his eleven-year-old son Baron next. He rightly pointed out the lopsided injustice. After a year of investigations with no evidence pointing to any crime, the media and Deep State continued to focus on Russia, Russia, Russia while ignoring very public and damning evidence pointing to crimes by Loretta Lynch, James Comey, Susan Rice, the Clinton Foundation and Hillary Clinton (e. g., destruction of emails under subpoena, destruction of a private server, hammers used on Blackberries and laptops, Bleach-bit, sale of twenty percent of the U. S.' uranium to Russia while Hillary served as Sec. of State and huge speaking fees paid to Bill Clinton, collusion between Ukraine and the Clinton campaign, etc.).

7/26/17: An aide to former DNC Chairwoman Debbie Wasserman Schultz, Imran Awan, was arrested for bank fraud while trying to flee to Lahore, Pakistan. Awan and other family members made a fortune providing IT services to Wasserman Schultz and other Democrat officials and politicians. As such, they had access to DNC laptops containing sensitive information. Fox News reported this story but it was largely ignored by the mainstream media. They continued to pound the Russia, Russia, Russia drum where no evidence had turned up after year-long, multiple investigations while ignoring this situation where serious criminal charges had been filed. Deplorables wondered if Awan might have been the source of DNC leaks to WikiLeaks and others.

SENATOR SUSAN COLLINS justified a possible Deplorable effort to primary her when the Maine RINO voted with six other GOP Senators and the Democrats against the straight repeal of Obamacare. At least Collins could say she was the only one of the seven who had never voted to repeal Obamacare under the previous administration.

RINO SENATORS LISA MURKOWSKI (AK), LAMAR ALEXANDER (TN), SHELLEY MOORE CAPITO (WV), DEAN HELLER (NV) and ROB PORTMAN (OH) flip-flopped and sided with the entire Democrat Caucus to defeat the straight repeal of Obamacare. These Senators had previously voted to repeal Obamacare when it didn't count because of the cover provided by then President Obama's veto power. These Senators had been elected on the promise to repeal Obamacare.

RINO SENATOR JOHN MCCAIN (AZ), an embittered Never-Trumper, flip-flopped and sided with the entire Democrat Caucus to defeat the straight repeal of Obamacare. The Senator had previously voted to repeal Obamacare when it didn't count because of the cover provided by then President Obama's veto power. The Senator had been elected on the promise to repeal Obamacare. Ironically, Arizona was one of the States that had been hit hardest by skyrocketing Obamacare premiums and deductibles. McCain's treachery was particularly galling since he had returned to the Senate days after surgery for a brain tumor and delivered a stirring speech to his colleagues to get off their duffs and get something done about healthcare.

President Trump faced a firestorm of criticism for courageously overturning President Obama's last minute attempt at social engineering at the expense of military effectiveness by announcing a ban on transgenders serving in the military. The mainstream media showered the public with fake statistics that made it seem like great numbers of transgenders formed the backbone of the U. S. Military. Tucker Carlson was excoriated for commenting that the job of the military was to win wars. No one defended the President by pointing out that transgenderism was considered a mental illness by many medical professionals. The media hammered away by citing a plethora of unsubstantiated heroic acts by transgender military members. No one cited the dangerous acts of treason committed by uber-leaker Bradley/Chelsea Manning.

During the televised White House Press Conference, Sarah Huckabee Sanders opened by reading a letter to President Trump from a nine-year-old boy named Dylan with the nickname of Pickle. Rather than accepting the heartwarming prose at face value, the feverish, conspiracy-frenzied media questioned the authenticity and spent an entire news cycle spinning wild theories about how the Trump Team contrived the whole matter. It turned out to be authentic but showed how desperate the media was to turn even the most positive news about President Trump into a negative.

7/27/17: Bruce/Caitlyn Jenner jumped off the Trump Train after the President announced the ban on transgender service in the military. The media fawned over the celebrity freak while Deplorables wondered when Caitlyn would put his money where his mouth was and have his man-parts surgically removed. Deplorables also scratched their heads and wondered how it would make the U. S. Military more effective by spending DOD dollars to anatomically change men into women and vice versa.

The mainstream media, Democrats who called Jeff Sessions a racist during his confirmation hearings and many moderate Republicans (Dems in disguise) rushed to defend the beleaguered Attorney General by claiming he had no ethical choice but to recuse himself from the Russia Investigation. Every one of these hypocrites had said nary a peep about Loretta Lynch's refusal to recuse herself from the Clinton Investigation even though she met privately with Bill Clinton during the investigation for over a half hour to supposedly chat about their grandkids and golf. By

Comey's own testimony before Congress, Lynch had also instructed the FBI Director to refer to the Clinton Investigation as a "matter" rather than an investigation.

The mainstream media, mentally ill liberals and many cowardly Republicans jumped on the bandwagon to condemn President Trump's decision to disallow transgenders in the military. The alligator tears flowed freely as they positioned his return to the U. S.' long-standing policy as a violation of human rights even insisting that the DOD should pay for their medical needs (swapping penises for vaginas).

Few if any had the courage to point out that serving in the military was not a right. In my day, everyone registered with the Selective Service. Even though we had voluntary service today rather than a draft, the military still reserved the right to be selective. Every day many people were denied the privilege of serving because of physical or mental deficiencies or the inability to meet strict standards including physical endurance. No one was whining for people who were too short, fat, weak or dumb to make the grade. The outcry for transgenders showed that their protests had nothing to do with military readiness and cost effectiveness but rather reflected a misguided attempt at social engineering that put the American people at risk.

SENATORS LISA MURKOWSKI and SUSAN COLLINS again sided with Democrats in assuring the American people would continue to be saddled with Obamacare by voting against even a "skinny repeal."

SENATOR JOHN MCCAIN cast the deciding vote that ensured America would continue to suffer egregiously under Obamacare. In an insanely ironic move, a vote on the measure had only been made possible by McCain risking his own health after major brain surgery by returning to Washington, D. C. to cast the deciding vote to allow for Senate debate on healthcare. After chiding his colleagues in a rousing speech for failing to take action, he appeared to stick a dagger in the backs of all Americans in order to satisfy his lust for vengeance against Donald Trump and killed the final chance to at least start the legislative demise of Obamacare. He cited his reason as a lack of trust in House Majority Leader Paul Ryan to make improvements during the House/Senate Conference phase as promised. This promise was accepted by other previous no voters: Senators Dean Heller, Rob Portman, Shelley Moore Capito and Lamar Alexander.

Fox's slide to the Left continued following the ouster of Roger Ailes in July 2016 and the shift of power from founder Rupert Murdoch to sons Lachlan and James Murdoch. Instead of fair and balanced, FNC leaned toward the anti-Trump crowd with Shepherd Smith leading the charge. No, this wasn't a meritless Deplorable conspiracy theory. After they assassinated Bill O'Reilly's career in April, bloodthirsty liberals tried to pull the same maneuver with Sean Hannity. He survived but this put the dwindling number of true conservatives at FNC on notice.

This was my Deplorable take on the state of affairs at **FNC** and the mindset of their various personalities as of this writing. The new FNC Show *Specialists* reversed the formula that made *The Five* successful (four conservatives or at least semi-conservatives surrounded one liberal). Liberal parrot **Eboni Williams** and squishy **Kat Timpf** formed bookends around token conservative **Eric Bolling**. When both guests were libs too, it was enough to make one switch the channel to watch reruns of Bonanza.

Juan Williams: When they pulled his string, he always praised or made excuses for Obama and robotically regurgitated the insane liberal talking points of the day.

Chris Wallace: FNC's sage was nothing but a closet liberal. Actually he wasn't in the closet at all … he became a real flamer!

Chris Stirewalt: The formerly great, straight-shooting analyst went over to the dark side. I didn't think he was a Never-Trumper but he appeared to think being anti-Trump could enhance his career prospects. He may have been right.

Charles Krauthammer: One of the brainiest guys on the planet let his inner Never-Trump out of its cage. In the process his gray matter turned to mush and it made me sad to see such great intellect and talent go to waste due to TDS.

Shepherd Smith: Deplorables demanded that he please go away. His show devolved into nothing more than a sixty-minute anti-Trump screed. NBC seemed to be calling for Shepherd to *please come home to where he belonged.* He needed to form a club with Megyn Kelly and Alisyn Camerota.

The Five moved into a new time slot other than five o'clock which made no sense. At least the conservatives still held sway with **Dana Perino** being a closet lib along with flamer **Juan**. Deplorables thanked God for **Jesse Watters, Kimberly Guilfoyle** and **Greg Gutfeld**. Gutfeld couldn't be labeled conservative or liberal but at least he was irreverent, truly funny and a caustic truth-teller.

With Bill O'Reilly gone, **Sean Hannity** had a lot of heavy lifting to do. Deplorables thanked God for **Tucker Carlson** ... and praised the Lord for **Ainsley Earhardt, Steve Doocy** and **Brian Kilmeade**.

Deplorables kept an eye on **Brett Baier**. He was the closest thing FNC had to an impartial anchor but seemed to be vulnerable to the PC crowd. Sometimes he appeared to lean a little left but, to his credit, he made both conservatives and liberals feel uncomfortable sometimes. Deplorables wanted to inoculate him with a tiny bit of Shepherd Smith's DNA to build up his immune system.

The best thing I could say about *Outnumbered* was that they were light-years better than *The View* which wasn't saying much. Nonetheless, Deplorables thanked God for **Harris Faulkner.**

Martha McCallum and **Bill Hemmer** were somewhat of a mystery. That was a good thing since, if they were closet liberals they didn't show it. They truly seemed to be fair and balanced without revealing any personal political leanings.

Jon Scott was always steady but perhaps needed a little more backbone and verve.

Cavuto was very good when he stuck to capitalism rather than moralizing about President Trump's tweets. At times he leaned like the Tower of Pisa.

Bottom line, despite their shortcomings, FNC represented about the only major outlet for at least partial truth and thus they continued to have a big target on their backs. Deplorables cherished FNC but wanted to see a shakeup at the top and an ouster of liberal ideologues and open flamers among the ranks. They thanked God that FNC still allowed great guests and contributors like Stuart Varney, General Jack Keane, Mark Steyn, Mark Levin, Dan Bongino, David Bossie, Corey Lewandowski, Sebastian Gorka, et al.

Media outlets reported that former Fox Host Megyn Kelly's ratings on NBC fell precipitously to a new low at less than half of the viewership she inherited there. At least Megyn Kelly showed her true colors by going to NBC which was more than we could say for many of the other closet liberals at FNC.

7/28/17: Charlie Gard died after being removed from life support. The eleven-month-old British baby became a victim of the British Healthcare System. Against the will of his parents, the government "death panel" decided not to seek experimental care for his rare genetic condition. When Charlie's parents objected, a protracted legal battle ensued while Charlie languished in a coma. The court finally ruled that Charlie should be allowed to seek experimental care from a U. S. physician who had successfully treated other such patients.

By the time the court finally ruled, Charlie's condition had deteriorated to where the parents had to acknowledge Charlie was beyond hope. This tragedy transpired just as Americans saw their hopes of ending Obamacare dashed. The death of little Charlie Gard offered a chilling glimpse into the future of government-run healthcare where bureaucrats and not doctors and patients made life or death decisions.

7/29/17: Rep. Barbara Lee referred to President Trump's newly named White House Chief of Staff John Kelly as an "extremist." Apparently, in her mind, a highly decorated Marine Corps General whose service to the United States included multiple combat tours in Iraq was unfit for duty in the White House. My suggestion was for Rep. Lee and her fellow

California Democrat colleague Maxine Waters to retire and start a business selling fruitcakes.

8/1/17: The NAACP issued a statewide travel advisory warning people of color against traveling to Missouri. This was done in response to the State Legislature's new law restricting frivolous discrimination lawsuits. Did people really look to the NAACP for travel advisories?

As if climate change hysteria wasn't wacky enough, NASA found a new way to waste our hard earned tax dollars. NASA posted a job opening for a Planetary Protection Officer with a salary of up to $187 thousand. Perhaps some thought that securing such protection against aliens was quite a bargain. Yes, wasn't this a small price to pay to ensure our compliance with the 1967 Outer Space Treaty? By the way, did the Martians sign this treaty? Supporters said this money was being spent to ensure that we didn't contaminate planets, moons and other objects in space.

8/2/17: CALEXIT gained momentum on the Left Coast. Yes, there was actually a serious movement calling for California to leave the United States to form their own country. As crazy as this sounded, it made perfect sense considering the insanity embraced by the majority of Californians. They had rejected federal immigration law, federal drug laws, capitalism, freedom of speech, the right to bear arms and the Christian religion. Deplorables felt that perhaps the United States should support the effort. If we removed U. S. military assets and assisted in relocating businesses and sane people to other states, there would be every reason to declare the new country of California a terrorist nation and impose stiff sanctions.

SMU forced students to remove a memorial consisting of three-thousand small American flags from the grounds in front of their main administrative building citing "triggering" concerns. What in the hell was triggering? Were they worried it might trigger patriotism? Were they concerned that students might remember the three-thousand Americans who were murdered by Muslim terrorists on 9/11? Thankfully, a landslide of outrage caused SMU to rethink their absurd policy.

ABC's narcissistic liberal loon, Jim Acosta, ranted against President Trump's proposed common sense immigration reform policy in front of the cameras during the White House Press Conference. He went so far as to infer President Trump was a racist who only wanted to allow immigration of English speaking people from Great Britain and Australia. The man at the podium, Presidential Advisor Stephen Miller, ripped Acosta a new one. He provided a history lesson about the Statue of Liberty and scolded Acosta for "cosmopolitan bias" in insinuating that only Brits and Aussies spoke English.

The Trump Administration and the American people continued to face serious threats such as N. Korea test firing ICBMs with the capability to reach the U. S. The Dow hit 22,000 for the first time; GDP growth kicked up to 2.6 percent and confidence in the economy gained momentum. What did the media focus on? They claimed President Trump lied when he said he'd received a call from the President of Mexico praising his crackdown on illegal immigration and calls from Boy Scout leaders about his recent speech to the organization. Sarah Huckabee Sanders explained that he misspoke in that the conversations were direct and not via the phone. So the fact that the conversations occurred as the President said didn't matter to the media. They parsed words and seized on a technicality regarding whether the talks occurred via phone or directly.

Realizing that their resistance campaign, Russian collusion hoax and so called Better Deal slogan weren't resonating with voters, Democrats tried to expand their party by hinting they would be open to pro-life candidates on their 2018 ticket. The leftist base of the party led by vocal proponents like Rosie O'Donnell immediately erupted in protest showing that Democrats had moved too far left to embrace a bigger tent movement. For them, being pro-death was still a litmus test.

8/3/17: Democrat Governor Jim Justice of West Virginia opened a Trump rally by announcing a switch to the Republican Party. He explained that he could no longer serve the people of West Virginia effectively as a Democrat because the party had drifted too far left.

8/4/17: Congress announced they were working on legislation to prohibit President Trump from firing Special Counsel Robert Mueller. This not only represented a usurpation of Executive Branch power but exhibited extreme bias and hypocrisy. They should have been taking steps to demand Mueller's removal for having a clear conflict of interest in sharing a close friendship with the star witness James Comey and hiring a phalanx of Clinton loyalists to serve in the investigation. The most disgusting aspect of this sordid, one-sided farce was that Deep State Republicans joined forces with Democrats to push for this legislation. **Deplorables took note of the need to clean house on the GOP side too in the primaries leading up to the 2018 elections.**

8/5/17: The insane liberal media had nothing better to do than criticize President Trump for taking his working vacation in New Jersey. I guess they felt he should have chosen a liberal bastion like President Obama did so many times in Cape Cod, Martha's Vineyard or Hawaii. By casting dispersions at the entire state of New Jersey, liberal elites continued to turn their noses up at people they considered DEPLORABLE.

The purge at Fox continued as FNC suspended Eric Bolling amid accusations that he sent lewd pictures of himself to female colleagues. He denied the allegations. Did evidence exist to corroborate the charges? It didn't appear so but one thing seemed certain. If a FNC anchor or host supported President Trump, inevitably they faced ouster attempts.

Atlanta gym owner Jim Chambers posted a sign barring police and veterans from using his gym. He cited rationale that it would make his minority clientele nervous to work out near cops.

8/8/17: Google fired software engineer James Damore after he published a memo critical of the company's diversity policy. He had the audacity to suggest that there were genetic differences between men and women.

GOP Senate Majority Leader Mitch McConnell had the nerve to blame President Trump's high expectations for making the Senate look bad. At a town hall meeting back in Kentucky, the do-nothing Senator said the President didn't understand how Washington worked and the amount of time required for passing legislation. He failed to mention that the Senate under his leadership hadn't accomplished anything in the first six months despite having received a mountain of legislation passed by the House. He also forgot his promise to have the Senate skip its August recess to get some work done.

When Kim Jong-un threatened to strike U. S. forces at Guam with a nuclear missile, President Trump sternly warned him that the U. S. would respond with "fire and fury." The mainstream media along with many Democrats and some Never-Trump Republicans criticized President Trump instead of North Korean madman Kim Jong-un. They called the President's threats unprecedented. This was quickly exposed as another lie by tapes that showed similarly stern threats had been issued by Presidents Clinton, Bush and Obama against the rogue regime. The only difference seemed to be that President Trump's words didn't represent a weak, hollow threat.

The saddest part of this latest anti-Trump tirade was that it showed the absence of a loyal opposition. The swamp dwellers sided with a totalitarian mass killer threatening nuclear war instead of supporting Donald Trump for even a minute. Guam's Governor, Eddie Calvo, welcomed President Trump's remarks saying he was glad to hear that an attack on U. S. citizens in Guam would be met with hell and fury.

8/9/17: FNC showed a clip from 1999 of then private citizen Donald Trump talking to Tim Russert about North Korea. The prescient businessman warned that North Korea would have nuclear tipped ICBMs that could reach the USA in a few years and cautioned that serious negotiations needed to commence immediately to stop them. Trump warned that it would be much more difficult to deal with North Korea once they gained the ability to deliver nukes against us. When faced with this threat, Presidents Bush and Obama had elected to kick the can down the road.

News outlets reported that Hillary Clinton was contemplating a new career as a pastor in the United Methodist Church. While wondering what was wrong with the United Methodist Church, I stayed tuned to the news for an update on whether hell had frozen over.

8/12/17: White supremacists clashed with violent, so called anti-fascists in Charlottesville, VA. President Trump made a public statement denouncing all forms of violence on all sides and offered a heartfelt plea for healing and unity. The media criticized the President for not singling out a particular group. It showed once again that the media would criticize President Trump no matter what he said or did.

The mainstream media had never criticized President Obama even though he had repeatedly rushed to judgment and had chosen sides on a variety of controversial matters thus deepening the divide in America. A case could be made that he had started the war on cops by calling the Cambridge Police stupid when he stuck his nose into the controversy involving his pal, Harvard Professor Henry Louis Gates.

The same media had also never criticized President Obama for not denouncing violence committed by leftist anarchists. President Obama had gone so far as to offer favorable views of Occupy Wall Street even when they rioted, burned and defecated in public. He had also provided moral support to BLM even when they had called for killing police. President Obama and the media had turned a blind eye to the wanton violence and destruction in Ferguson, Baltimore and elsewhere.

8/14/17: President Trump clarified his earlier remarks about the violence in Charlottesville, VA and specifically called out the KKK and other white supremacists as his critics demanded. Did this satisfy them? No, the liberal media continued their rant and now claimed that the statement hadn't come soon enough. This showed once again that Trump-haters would not be satisfied by anything done by the President short of his death or resignation from office.

President Trump interrupted his working vacation in NJ to visit Trump Tower in NY. He was greeted by a phalanx of paid, professional protesters/anarchists who hurled some of the most disgusting invectives imaginable. Of course the mainstream media lauded them.

Chicago Bear football player and noted sage Kyle Long lectured the American people about violence in the aftermath of the Charlottesville riots. Then he went to football practice and had to be removed after getting into several fights with his own teammates.

Violent anarchists in Durham, NC tore down the statue of a Confederate soldier while police turned a blind eye. Just days after denouncing one side responsible for the violence in Charlottesville (not Anti-Fa or BLM terrorists), the media didn't offer any criticism. In fact, they lauded the lawbreakers.

8/15/17: After weeks of the media denouncing President Trump for his fiery rhetoric toward North Korea, Kim Jong-un announced that, after talking to his military advisors, he decided not to attack Guam. Did the media laud President Trump for his tough, effective diplomacy in getting the Korean dictator to blink like Nikita Khrushchev? No, apparently diverting a nuclear war didn't warrant their praise or notice.

8/16/17: President Trump tried to hold a press conference to talk about improving America's crumbling infrastructure but the rabid dogs in the media only wanted to criticize him for Charlottesville again. President Trump fired back and made the mistake of telling the truth that both sides in the riot were guilty of unacceptable violence. He also criticized the lunatics who wanted to tear down monuments and eradicate American history. He asked, what's next … do we remove the Washington

Monument and Jefferson Memorial? The President was roundly denounced by the media and a host of hypocritical Republicans for telling the truth.

Tonight Show host Jimmy Fallon opened his show with a full display of his left-wing bias by predictably chastising President Trump for his comments on Charlottesville. Then he went way over the line by lecturing Trump's supporters. In effect, he called all sixty-two million Trump voters DEPLORABLE. Jimmy needed to stick to comedy since his political propaganda lacked any hint of humor.

8/17/17: Missouri State Senator Maria Chappelle-Nadal posted on Facebook that she hoped President Trump would be assassinated. This reflected the "tolerant" Left.

CNN commentator Angela Rye called for statues of slave owners George Washington and Thomas Jefferson to be destroyed. Hmmm ... was Donald Trump a prophet too?

While mentally ill, whiney, snowflake leftists in the U. S. busied themselves with the eminent danger presented by historical statues, ISIS-inspired terrorists in Barcelona used a rented van to mow down dozens of people enjoying a stroll along the popular Las Ramblas tourist district. Several mainstream media commentators including some of the liberals on FNC equated the Charlottesville attack with Barcelona. Democrats and the media called for a ban on rental vans ... NOT!

8/18/17: The news media trumpeted Barcelona's pluck and resolve by showing the outpouring of support provided in the form of useless rhetoric as had been done in the innumerable preceding attacks. The feckless West continued to crow about resiliency while the death toll climbed higher and higher. Talking heads wondered aloud how we could get at the root cause while virtually no one called for a counter-offensive against the real root cause; the evil ideology of the Islamists.

8/19/17: For months the mainstream media had led the calls for Strategist Steve Bannon to be banished from the West Wing. When President Trump forced his resignation, the Left lauded President Trump for his wise, responsive leadership ... NOT! As with the firing of FBI Director James Comey, liberals and the media roundly criticized President Trump for giving them what they wanted.

Just a week prior, liberal loons had excoriated President Trump for denouncing the violence coming from both sides in the Charlottesville riots. The media had howled that he was supporting white supremacists by declaring BLM and Anti-Fa complicit in the violence. In Boston, a group of peaceful protestors held a legally licensed rally in support of freedom of speech. Anti-Fa came out in their black masks and jack boots to oppose the freedom of speech rally. They threw rocks and urine on the peaceful protesters and in one instance even knocked down an elderly woman while yanking the American flag out of her hands.

How could they oppose free speech and intimidate a small crowd of largely elderly citizens at a legally-licensed, peaceful rally??? Did the media denounce Anti-Fa and the anarchists? No, they still tried to portray them as noble, heroic figures. Deplorables felt that Anti-Fa fascists should be called Anti-Pa ... anti-patriotic.

8/20/17: USC's mascot, the Trojan, had been celebrated for decades while riding into football games on a horse. Left-wing loons noticed that the famous Trojan's horse was named Traveller which coincidentally was the name of one of Robert E. Lee's favorite steeds and called for the statue of the horse to be removed from campus.

8/21/17: Left-wing loons called for an alternate exhibit to be added to the Jefferson Memorial in Washington, D. C. to depict his life as a slave owner. Unbelievably, this suggestion received serious consideration by lawmakers including spineless Republicans.

Even some Democrats, including Sen. Claire McCaskill who was nervous about her re-election campaign, called for MO State Sen. Maria Chappelle-Nadal to resign over her call for President Trump's assassination. She refused to resign and then, under pressure, offered an apology and cited her Christianity as justification for her not doing the right and honorable thing. She called herself a servant of God. Liberals stood by her despite her self-confessed "mistake" while continuing their hate-filled assault on President Trump.

Delusional "moderates" on both sides of the aisle used the total solar eclipse as an occasion for everyone to sing *Kumbaya* and come together as a nation. One could have substituted the term insane for delusional. That was because no one even hinted at acknowledging the root cause of our great national divide: identity politics that purposefully pitted one group against another for political gain.

8/23/17: The mentally ill liberals at ESPN pulled their Asian-American announcer from an upcoming University of Virginia football game because they feared people in Virginia would be upset that he coincidentally shared the same name, Robert Lee, as the Confederate General.

St. Louis Mayor Lyda Krewson kept up her insane crusade against statues and monuments by having the pavement removed from the street in Forest Park known as Confederate Way. In the meantime, businesses continued to flee while St. Louis remained one of the murder capitals of the world.

8/24/17: Wild-eyed liberal Mayor Bill DeBlasio of NYC called for the removal of the statue of Christopher Columbus and Grant's Tomb. Yes, that Grant ... the Union General who led the North to victory in the Civil War and later served as President of the United States. Those accomplishments were apparently overshadowed by some anti-Semitic comments he supposedly made.

Liberals, the media and establishment Republicans went berserk in criticizing President Trump for declaring that he might shut down the government if the Congress didn't include funding for the southern border wall in the upcoming budget bill. Somehow, they all forgot how President Obama had used the same tactic to coerce the Congress into passing a clean resolution without any spending cuts the last time they raised the nation's debt limit.

During a protest against the killing of a transgender woman who had stabbed a police officer, an angry mob attacked a driver who tried to pass through the St. Louis intersection they had illegally blocked. They pounded his car with their fists and pipes and three people jumped on his vehicle. He honked his horn to no avail and then, in obvious fear for his life, slowly accelerated to escape the mob. In the process, the three people on top of his car fell to the ground and sustained minor injuries. The police did nothing to the lawbreakers but arrested the driver on a felony charge.

D. James Kennedy's Christian Ministry Group filed a defamation lawsuit against the Southern Poverty Law Center after the disingenuous Progressive organization added the Christian ministry to its list of hate groups for espousing biblical teachings on sexuality and marriage.

Former House Speaker Newt Gingrich drew a parallel between the media's unhinged reaction to Donald Trump and the South's reaction to the inauguration of Abraham Lincoln. He hinted of his fear of a new civil war by saying that it appeared the Left would only get crazier and crazier.

8/25/17: Liberals continued to occupy their time with the status of former NFL quarterback and erstwhile protestor Colin Kaepernick while Trump-haters of every stripe continued to block the people's agenda for better healthcare, a secure border, lower taxes and jobs, jobs, jobs.

Deplorables grew sick and tired of seeing miniscule but hyper-vocal minorities drive America's agenda with the aid of the media's megaphone. The vast majority of Americans did not want to see historical monuments, including those of the Founding Fathers, torn down or defaced. Most people grew weary of hearing about transgender complaints and bathroom issues. Hordes of people wanted to vomit over political correctness as it soared to insane new levels. Deplorables of every color grew sick and tired of the race card being played over and over and over.

A first grader in a California charter school was sent to the principal's office for "bullying" a transgender student. The first grader didn't realize that her classmate, a boy, had decided to become a girl. Unaware, she called him by his boy name rather than his new girl name. This was deemed bullying and the girl had to go to the principal's office for counseling that left her afraid and confused.

8/27/17: Conservatives attempted to hold a peaceful rally in Berkeley, CA to promote free speech. They were confronted by Anti-Fa anarchists in black masks carrying clubs and pepper spray. The one-sided violence was captured on video and police arrested over a dozen Anti-Fa anarchists. Even some Democrats denounced Anti-Fa but the mainstream media still gave them a pass. Conservatives called for Anti-Fa to be added to the federal list of terrorist organizations.

Kenneth Storey, Assistant Professor of Sociology at the University of Tampa, demonstrated how truly hateful and intolerant people on the hard Left were by tweeting that Hurricane Harvey represented karma against Trump supporters in Texas. Not only was his theology horribly screwed up but he apparently forgot about all of the Democrats and Hillary supporters that Harvey indiscriminately pounded as it hit Texas and Louisiana. Such a backlash occurred that the University fired Storey two days later.

8/28/17: Illinois GOP Governor Bruce Rauner caved in to the liberal pressure he'd been facing since his inauguration as the blue state's last, best hope for true reform. After passing a series of loony leftist legislative bills, he put the last nail in his coffin by approving legislation making Illinois a sanctuary state. It left supporters wondering if he'd gone mad. By alienating his base did he really think he could count on Democrats for re-election?

8/29/17: So called activists … some of the same ilk who looted and burned down parts of Ferguson, MO … threatened to shut down St. Louis unless a federal judge found former St. Louis Police Officer Jason Stockley guilty of the murder of Anthony Lamar Smith in the line of duty on December 20, 2011. Prosecutors alleged that Stockley planted a gun in the dead victim's car to justify the shooting.

Originally, no charges were brought since no evidence existed to support the claim. The case was reopened, apparently for political reasons, even though no new evidence was brought to bear. In Ferguson the violence had erupted in <u>reaction</u> to a not guilty verdict against Officer Darrin Wilson in the shooting of Michael Brown. In this case, the same type of mob violence was threatened <u>before</u> the verdict in an effort to influence the outcome.

Pathetic comedienne Kathy Griffin had offered her weak non-apology apology back on 5/31/17 for posing in a picture while holding a bloody likeness of President Trump's severed head. On this day, she came back and officially revoked her apology and claimed to be the victim. In one fell swoop she proved herself not only to be a hater but disingenuous and stupid too. She could be excused though since she suffered from TDS.

8/30/17: The Trump Administration's response to Hurricane Harvey was so well organized and proactive that it left the media and his haters with little to complain about. In fact, they grew so tired of posting images of Texans and other Americans coming together in unity and love to help Harvey's victims that they turned their sights on the First Lady. With nothing negative to report, the media created a tempest in a teapot by slamming Melania Trump for wearing high heels during her trip to Texas with the President to offer hope and encouragement to the storm ravaged victims. They even had to lie in the process since Mrs. Trump didn't actually wear high heels on the tour of Corpus Christi. She wore the stiletto heels while boarding Air Force One but then changed into her sneakers before deplaning in Texas.

Anti-Fa's behavior became so obviously abhorrent that even Nancy Pelosi had to denounce their violence. Why didn't former President Obama follow suit? Maybe he didn't want to draw attention to the fact that he had invited some of their BLM peers to the White House after committing similarly violent acts in Ferguson and Baltimore. In any case, amidst growing calls for Anti-Fa to be added to the list of terrorist organizations in the U. S., the mainstream media continued to give them a pass.

9/5/17: Illegals held protests at Trump Tower and across the land and the haters in the mainstream media denounced President Trump for his lack of compassion in ending DACA; President Obama's executive order that granted amnesty and federal benefits to so called Dreamers or children whose parents brought them to the United States illegally.

Taking all of the emotion (liberal hatred) out of the equation, liberals overlooked these facts. President Obama, by his own admission, violated the

Constitution in enacting immigration law apart from the Congress. President Trump faced a deadline since the executive order was set to expire and ten States Attorneys General had filed suit to end DACA. Sane legal scholars agreed almost unanimously that DACA violated the Constitution. Conservatives pressed for President Trump to end DACA immediately by executive fiat which was his right. President Trump showed true compassion toward the Dreamers by granting a six-month extension while pressuring Congress to do their job and enact comprehensive immigration reform.

9/10/17: On the Sunday news shows to promote her new book of excuses for her 2016 loss, Hillary Clinton blamed "millions of white people" and thus again effectively declared Trump's basket of Deplorables to be racists.

9/12/17: Irresponsible Congressman Luis Gutierrez (Dem, IL) declared Gen. John Kelly to be a disgrace to the uniform because he allowed President Trump to end DACA. Deplorables tried to unpack this insanity. Did Gutierrez really believe that General Kelly and not the President called the shots? Was he upset because the President decided to follow the law rather than legislating from the Oval Office? Did he really expect President Trump to continue with President Obama's executive order that almost every legal scholar had agreed was unconstitutional? Couldn't he see the compassion in President Trump's decision to let DACA stand for six months while Congress did their job? Did he really believe John Kelly disgraced the uniform by serving in the Marines in combat, rising through the ranks and leading our troops in battle ... and in losing his own son in combat while serving our nation?

Black female ESPN analyst Jemele Hill issued the following racist rant on Twitter, "Donald Trump is a white supremacist who has largely surrounded himself w/ other white supremacists." ESPN tacitly condoned her words by issuing no punishment other than a weak verbal reprimand saying her statement didn't represent ESPN's position. This revealed ESPN's grossly liberal bias when compared to how they treated Curt Shilling's conservative social media post in April 2016 when the former MLB pitcher and ESPN analyst was fired for opposing transgender bathroom laws that allowed biological males to use female restrooms. If anyone had any doubts about ESPN's liberal lunacy, Colin Kaepernick cleared up any confusion by coming out publicly in support of Jemele Hill.

9/13/17: Jimmy Carter, former worst president in U. S. history before Barack Obama, came out of obscurity to criticize President Trump and urged him to seek peace with Kim Jong-un. Deplorables excused Carter on the basis of senility but not the media who trumpeted his words as if coming from a sage on high.

Deplorables received proof positive of the importance of their 2016 victory when the new Supreme Court with Justice Neil Gorsuch in place temporarily struck down the liberal lower court restrictions on President Trump's travel ban. Sanity finally prevailed in favor of the nation's security. Unfortunately, the Supreme Court's final ruling in October remained academic since the ninety-day travel ban had already expired by then.

9/14/17: Hillary Clinton called for an end to the Electoral College. More than any other year, 2016 reflected the wisdom of our Electoral College system. She lost in thirty of the fifty States. Hillary won the popular vote by over-indexing in California. Take that away and she lost the popular vote too. Why should the rest of the U. S. suffer through a Hillary Clinton presidency because of such a small minority of States led by the Left Coast loons in California? Deplorables hadn't forgotten that the popular vote was still in question with Democrats continuing to withhold data showing an incredible amount of voter fraud. How many millions of non-citizens had voted???

9/17/17: Out of town anarchists including BLM and Anti-Fa descended upon St. Louis to "protest" the judge's decision to acquit former police officer Jason Stockley who had shot and killed Anthony Lamar Smith in 2011 in the line of duty. Smith who had prior convictions for selling drugs and illegally possessing weapons resisted arrest, crashed his car into Stockley's squad car and sped away at speeds of up to ninety mph. After a high speed chase through the city streets, Stockley ordered Smith to exit the car with his hands up. Smith refused and, according to Stockley, appeared to reach for a gun. Stockley fired five shots and killed Smith. They found heroin and a gun in Smith's car.

The prosecutors argued that Stockley planted the gun even though video evidence didn't back up the claim. "Protesters" including some clergy had tried to pressure the judge into a guilty verdict by threatening to "shut the city down" if he issued an acquittal. Thankfully, the judge courageously resisted mob rule and ruled according to the evidence. With the media fanning the flames, the "protesters" made good on their threats. As expected, the "peaceful protests" turned violent and destructive after nightfall.

Throughout the weekend, the anarchists moved throughout the City and County attacking various targets. They tried to block highway exits and intersections near Barnes Jewish Hospital. Did they really want to make their point by endangering the lives of people needing emergency medical attention? They mobbed West County Mall. This showed their true colors. They didn't care about the impact on regular people trying to shop and work. This equated to an attack on capitalism and free commerce.

In a move reminiscent of Hitler's Brown Shirts, they vandalized and broke the windows of a public library. They marauded through University City's

Delmar Loop and vandalized some twenty businesses. These people had nothing to do with the Stockley decision. Again the "protesters" proved their disdain for small business people and free market capitalism.

Numerous high school football games had to be cancelled along with a U2 concert and other events. Yet, the people of St. Louis continued to elect Democrats after fifty years of mismanagement and steady decline. All of this angst poured out over what the court ruled to be a legally justified shooting of a criminal while the people ignored St. Louis's unfortunate but well-earned reputation as one of the nation's murder capitals due to black-on-black crime. Where was the outrage over the daily deaths of all these innocents?

The Emmy Awards became a political rally for left-wing loons. I didn't watch it but unfortunately caught some of the vile shenanigans in subsequent news clips. They even trotted out Hanoi Jane to make rude, disgusting remarks about the President. They wondered why ratings were down. Deplorables offered a clue. The majority of Americans wanted to be entertained by actors, musicians and athletes. They didn't want to be bombarded with their unhinged political opinions.

9/18/17: California passed new legislation making it a sanctuary state. This was the state that gave Hillary Clinton the edge in the popular vote in 2016. They were more concerned with protecting illegal immigrants than their own, law-abiding citizens … insanity!

Police in London arrested Yahyah Farroukh and another young man in connection with an alleged terrorist attack where they set off a bomb on a subway train. Early reports indicated that the terrorists were refugees from Iraq who had been welcomed into Great Britain with open arms. Their foster parents, Penelope and Ronald Jones, had even been personally honored by the Queen for their humanitarianism.

This shed new light on the insanity of Europe's open border policies. It also showed the dastardly minds of the nefarious radical Islamic terrorists. This was the way they showed their thanks for being rescued by the charitable Brits. They set off a bomb on a subway train full of innocent people. Thankfully, the bomb didn't detonate fully but still left about twenty people injured, some with severe burns.

9/20/17: After President Trump's stirring speech at the U. N. where he put North Korea and Iran on notice, Hillary Clinton and John Kerry came out in criticism of the President. They scolded him for not carrying on with the same feckless diplomacy they and others had employed for the past twenty years to get us into such a mess. Deplorables wondered why they wouldn't just go away. They silently chanted *drain the swamp*!

St. Louis Mayor Lyda Krewson accused the police chief of being inflammatory when he reassured people that the cops would not yield the streets to the thugs posing as protesters. This was after the "protesters" vandalized Lyda Krewson's home and continued to come out night after night with endless violence and vandalism that hearkened back to the Ferguson riots. Then Mayor Krewson showed how she'd lost all common sense to political posturing when she said she still had confidence in the police chief even though she'd just thrown him under the bus. Liberalism was truly a mental illness on full display.

Eric Greitens had been elected Governor of Missouri in 2016 by running as a supposedly tough, no nonsense ex-Navy Seal who would not tolerate former Governor Nixon's appeasement policy toward the Ferguson rioters. Some had wondered about his true nature during his campaign when he was the only conservative running in the GOP primary that came out in favor of insane liberal bathroom policies.

As Governor, he had shown his true colors by giving State Rep. Maria Chappelle-Nadal a pass. After her calls for President Trump to be assassinated, Governor Greitens had vowed to have her removed from the State Senate but then became a coward and let her off with a meaningless censure. He erased any doubt about his lack of conviction when the St. Louis riots broke out. Although he had put the National Guard on notice, there was no sign of them after many days of looting and vandalism. He apparently decided to keep them on the sidelines while businesses and the people of St. Louis suffered at the hands of professional thugs. St. Louis's already damaged national image suffered more irreparable harm due to his inaction.

Deplorables had a message for the Governor ... *hello ... the people in the City of St. Louis didn't vote for you! Why were you trying to appease the liberals who would never vote for you under any circumstances by alienating the people who put you in office?*

9/23/17: Hillary Clinton continued her endless excuse tour. She scolded white women for not seeing the threat from Donald Trump. Then she went on to resurrect her delusional, vast right-wing conspiracy. This time she chastised the Founders for including the Fifth Amendment in the Constitution because it gave the States, the people, the right to curb the power of the federal government. Deplorables begged for somebody to please make her go away.

9/24/17: President Trump spoke for all Deplorable sports fans when he called for NFL brats refusing to stand for the national anthem before games to be fired. He courageously called out all of the whiny millionaire posers who claimed to be fighting oppression. This brought back recollections of Colin Kaepernick claiming to be combating oppression while wearing a Fidel Castro t-shirt. Perhaps Colin and his ignorant cohorts should have moved to Cuba and gained a real education in oppression.

This time around, NFL hypocrites claimed to be taking a stand on behalf of freedom of speech while they denounced President Trump for exercising his First Amendment rights. They had the nerve to claim President Trump's words were divisive while doing everything possible to divide the country along political lines. Now we couldn't even enjoy sports without getting thrown into a political scrum. President Trump spoke for fans everywhere by stating, in effect, that athletes and entertainers should perform without subjecting audiences to their political opinions.

I was most disappointed by one of my former heroes, Kurt Warner. He had given me an uneasy feeling earlier during his Hall of Fame induction speech. It lacked the humility and sincerity of the old Kurt Warner. It came across as almost arrogant and self-centered. Warner confirmed my fears and erased any doubts by supporting the anarchists out of, I guessed, political correctness and cowardice. He called kneeling and disrespecting our flag, nation and veterans an "honorable" form of free speech while chastising President Trump for exercising his right to free speech. I grieved over such behavior from someone I'd looked to as a Christian role model. Apparently, no one was immune to TDS.

The "protests" continued across the St. Louis area. How long could this possibly carry on: weeks, months, years? The targets continued to be malls, businesses, concert venues and people and locations that had nothing to do with the shooting of Anthony Lamar Smith. This all tied in with the ongoing national narrative calling vaguely for social justice and an end to oppression.

What did this mean? Could anyone tell us what specific actions were necessary to end the madness? What kind of freedom was needed? Did they mean the freedom to try to ruin kids' lives by selling drugs, running down police officers with cars, crashing cars into police vehicles and endangering innocent lives by escaping through city streets at ninety mph and then attempting to pull a gun on a police officer without consequence? Did they mean the freedom to rob a convenience store, rough up the proprietor, pummel a police officer and attempt to wrestle away his gun to shoot him without consequence? Did they mean the ability of street gangs to engage in shootouts where stray bullets killed innocent girls and grandmothers hiding in their homes without consequence? Did they mean the ability of teen thugs to sneak up on senior citizens and knock them silly or dead playing the knock-out game while targeting people on the basis of skin color without consequence?

Where was the outrage for all of the black lives snuffed out in Chicago and elsewhere by black gunmen? Did anyone remember the names of those victims like they did with Michael Brown, Freddie Gray or Anthony Lamar Smith? Was anyone taking a knee for them? Had anyone ever considered that the "oppression" of inner city dwellers might have had something to do with the Democrats who had been in charge of our major cities for over fifty years? No, they continued to vote them into office while distracted by shiny objects … it was those darned statues that were causing all the problems.

9/25/17: Hillary Clinton continued her excuse tour on MSNBC and … surprise; surprise … played the race card in addressing the NFL protests. She claimed Donald Trump was attacking black athletes when he scolded players for taking a knee during the national anthem. Deplorables were SO TIRED of Democrats playing the race card over and over and over again. They couldn't engage in a meaningful debate on the basis of policy so they resorted to name calling and ultimately, always their favorite label if you disagreed with them: racist.

9/27/17: Former First Lady Michelle Obama came out publicly to criticize women who voted for Donald Trump by saying they didn't respect their own voices. This conformed perfectly with the divisive identity politics promoted by her husband and fellow Democrats. Translation: If you were a woman who didn't vote for Hillary because she was a woman, then you were out of the club and if you were a black who didn't vote Democrat then you were a traitor to your community and not really black. Whatever happened to Martin Luther King Jr's call to judge people on the content of their character and not the color of their skin … or gender for that matter?

9/28/17: One of the bluest states, Massachusetts, provided us with another example of liberal lunacy. In an effort to promote reading among grade school children, First Lady Melania Trump donated some Dr. Seuss books to school districts all around the country. Liz Phipps Soeiro, a librarian for the Cambridge, MA Public Schools, refused to accept the gift and called Seuss' books "racist propaganda."

Apparently, if you enjoyed books like *Horton Hears a Who*, *Green Eggs and Ham* or *The Cat in the Hat* as a kid, you were a brainwashed racist. Who could have guessed that the seemingly erudite, uniquely imaginative, grandfatherly Theodor Seuss Geisel was the evil mastermind behind the white supremacy that had gripped America? As we'd seen before, TDS extended to the whole Trump family, even including eleven-year-old Barron. Did we really want people teaching our children who were so blinded by hatred that they would refuse a gift of Dr. Seuss classics?

9/29/17: Ever wonder why St. Louis went from one of the nation's thriving metropolises as the Gateway to the West to a national laughingstock? It boiled down to fifty years of Democrat control. For example, the current Board of Aldermen considered a resolution recognizing and praising the work of the St. Louis Police but it had to be mothballed in committee review due to pressure from the never-ending "protesters." This unfathomable nonsense was rendered truly insane in light of the resolution passed the week before by the same Board. They honored Anthony Lamar Smith for his many lifetime accomplishments which included continuing his informal education through reading and listening to music. Translation: he didn't pursue formal education after a nondescript trip through high school.

The resolution also lamented a life cut short of someone who wanted to help kids. St. Louis's Deplorables gagged as the Board of Aldermen honored a heroin dealer who had built a long rap sheet and ruined countless lives while profiting off other people's misery. When caught in the act by police, he tried to run them down, rammed their car and took off on a high speed getaway through the streets of St. Louis. When finally apprehended, he reportedly went for his gun and got shot to death in the process. The courts acquitted the officer who shot him. It was appropriate to mourn the dead under any circumstances but not to conjure up sainthood.

9/30/17: San Juan's Mayor, Carmen Yulin Cruz, stood out like a sore thumb in leveling criticism at President Trump and his administration in the wake of Hurricane Maria. The governor of Puerto Rico and many others there along with officials in Texas, Louisiana and Florida had nothing but praise for the relief efforts. President Trump was excoriated by the media when he fired back at Cruz for politicizing the crisis. Then her true motives were revealed by top FEMA officials who reported that Mayor Cruz had not visited or contacted the FEMA relief headquarters in San Juan. She had time to acquire a special hat and t-shirt with her slanted political rhetoric and appeared on numerous cable news broadcasts but somehow couldn't find the time to visit the FEMA headquarters in her own city to try to help coordinate the relief efforts.

10/1/17: Pennsylvania State University – Brandywine Professor Angela Putnam called hard work and meritocracy a white ideology. She openly taught her students to deplore the whiteness of the false notion that successful people got there through their own hard work. Deplorables thought the racist professor needed to look in the mirror. Did she really think a strong work ethic was exclusive to whites? People paid good money and kids left college with massive debt so they could learn that hard work was a bad, racist notion. I was not joking when I repeated that liberalism had become a mental illness.

10/2/17: How come the mainstream media didn't say a peep about the corruption trial of NJ Senator Robert Menendez? Oh yeah, he was a Democrat.

We awoke to the horrific news of a gunman perched on the thirty-second floor of the Mandalay Bay Hotel in Las Vegas opening fire on an outdoor country music festival below. The initial body count included over fifty killed and more than four-hundred wounded. Americans wondered if this terrible tragedy would bring us together and stop the insane, meaningless, petty protesting by anarchists in St. Louis and elsewhere. The short, simple and unfortunate answer was no. Within hours of the shootings, before the body count even ended, while hundreds lay in hospitals and volunteers gave blood to save lives, the Democrats led by Hillary Clinton politicized the mass murder by bellowing their gun control mantra. Deplorables cried out again for Hillary to just go away!

The *Monday Night Football* game between Kansas City and the Redskins provided more evidence of the great divide in America when the announcer dedicated the national anthem to the victims of the carnage in Las Vegas. Surely everyone stood, right? No, Marcus Peters of the Chiefs decided to sit down anyway. The next evening in St. Louis, the anarchists/protesters couldn't take a night off to show some sympathy toward the victims in Las Vegas. Over two-hundred arrests were made as these miscreants tried to shut down Interstate 64.

CBS Legal Executive Haley Geftman-Gold said in the wake of the Las Vegas massacre that "I'm actually not even sympathetic [because] country music fans often are Republican gun toters." Amid a firestorm of criticism from all directions, CBS fired Geftman-Gold. Although I abhorred her sentiments, I felt it was hypocritical to fire her since she had only been honest. If others at CBS and elsewhere had been equally as honest, they would have admitted that they too felt that justice had been served. This kind of hatred had become the norm for liberals. If someone disagreed with them, they thought they should be silenced and ultimately put to death. That's why they lauded violent, anarchistic groups like BLM and Anti-Fa.

10/3/17: The media continued to report that the Las Vegas mass murderer, Stephen Paddock, had no apparent motive for his actions. I stuck my neck out and said this guy wasn't crazy and didn't just fly off the handle. Had he become radicalized through his girlfriend? Radical Islamic terrorism surely should have been considered as a motive even though, perhaps, he'd covered his tracks by not using social media. Why were the authorities so quick to deny any ties to the Muslim terrorists without having all the facts at their disposal?

CNN Reporter Jeff Zeleny, while reporting on the Las Vegas massacre, felt the need to comment that most of the victims were likely Trump supporters. Although sick, Zeleny deserved perverse credit for being honest like Haley Geftman-Gold. Liberals were so deranged that they saw conservatism and especially support of President Trump as an offense punishable by death.

It seemed that many liberals saw the victims as the perpetrators and the shooter as the victim. Drexel University Professor George Ciccariello-Maher (why do so many libs have hyphenated names?) said that "extreme Trumpism" and "white victimization" motivated the Las Vegas shooter, Stephen Paddock. First, it was quite interesting that the professor somehow had figured out the shooter's motivation while the FBI and others remained baffled. Second, I wondered if this dork would eat his words if Paddock was found to have been radicalized. Folks, Ciccariello-Maher and so many others like him were teaching our kids!

10/5/17: Nancy Pelosi shocked many conservatives by actually telling the truth. As the gun control debate raged, Democrats found a crack in the GOP's armor by pushing for a common sense ban on bump stocks (approved by President Obama's ATF) that effectively turned semi-automatic weapons into something akin to automatic weapons. A reporter asked her if this move was just a slippery slope toward the elimination of gun ownership and she said yes; she hoped it would create a slippery slope.

The wicked-witch-who-wouldn't-go-away, Hillary Clinton, continued to thrust herself upon Americans who had soundly rejected her and she refused to relinquish her erstwhile role as the leader of the Democrats. She remained in the lead on the gun control debate and ratcheted up the dangerous, partisan rhetoric by claiming that the NRA and GOP were responsible for the Las Vegas mass murder.

10/6/17: Rep. Tim Murphy of PA announced his pending resignation after news broke that the supposedly pro-life Republican encouraged his mistress to seek an abortion when he thought she was pregnant. This was important because it illustrated what we needed to do to achieve a Deplorable victory in 2018. It was more than just ousting liberal Democrats.

Deplorables needed to rid our government of liberals and establishment elites posing as conservatives. This included people like Susan Collins, Lisa Murkowski and John McCain who posed as moderate Republicans but then regularly voted as if members of the Democrat Caucus. John McCain used to be different since, as a lukewarm RINO, he held to a mixture of conservative and liberal beliefs. But after contracting TDS, he eschewed some of his previously held conservative positions and screwed the American people in order to exact his vengeful retribution against Donald Trump.

Fox News reported that the media's coverage of President Trump during his first nine months in office was ninety-two percent negative and eight percent positive. Other studies showed the coverage not quite that slanted but even liberal pundits and pollsters agreed that the coverage tilted far to the negative side, much worse than predecessors Obama, Bush and Clinton had received during their first years in office. Outside of Fox News, hardly a peep was said about some of the amazingly positive results achieved by the Trump Administration: lowest unemployment numbers in over a decade, a record high stock market, significant reductions in our trade imbalances and soaring consumer confidence.

Deplorable viewers didn't need to see these statistics to know the truth. All they had to do was turn on any White House Press Conference and listen to the barrage of biased, nasty, disrespectful questions hurled at Sarah Huckabee Sanders. If that wasn't enough, they saw how the media nit-picked every syllable from President Trump and First Lady Melania as they visited storm-ravaged Texas, Florida and Puerto Rico and the victims suffering from Stephen Paddock's rampage in Las Vegas. They ignored the heartfelt consolation offered by the President and looked for any excuse to paint him as uncaring and slow to respond.

The media even spitefully criticized Thomas Gunderson, one of the victims of the Las Vegas shooter. When President Trump came to visit the wounded man in the hospital, Gunderson refused to stay in bed and struggled to stand up out of respect and gratitude toward the President. Deplorables saw this as more proof that liberalism had become a mental illness.

Senate Minority Leader Chuck Schumer had the unmitigated gall to supposedly speak for the Las

Vegas shooting victims. He claimed to have apparently channeled the dead by declaring that the deceased victims who were in heaven wanted President Trump to do something about gun control. This went far beyond his normally disgusting politicization of the issue. He not only arrogantly presumed to know the political views of people he had never met but how they may have adjusted their perspective after being murdered.

A few muted conservative voices picked up on this outrageous behavior but no one noticed the theological quotient. Schumer declared that all of the victims were in heaven. Really Chuck, you knew they were in heaven? Why didn't someone ask him to explain his theology in depth? How did they get to heaven? Did they all have faith in Jesus Christ as their Savior? Or were you implying the eternally dangerous, false teaching that all steeples pointed up and everyone went to heaven regardless of what they believed? Deplorables thought Reverend Chuck needed to get a clue before turning his political podium into a pulpit.

10/8/17: Vice President Mike Pence left a NFL game between the Indianapolis Colts and San Francisco Forty Niners after a dozen of the latter's players kneeled during the national anthem. As if on cue, the lamestream media criticized the VP. With nothing else to hang their hat on, the Democrats, at the height of hypocrisy, scolded Pence for spending taxpayer dollars to travel to Indianapolis. Yes, the tax and spend kings and queens of waste used that one. Hello, McFly ... since when was it okay to denigrate our flag and everything it stood for but unacceptable to take a stand in its defense? Deplorables lamented ... *only in America* ... as we shook our collective heads.

10/9/17: Frank Sinatra had died almost twenty years prior so, of course, a derogatory remark he made toward Donald Trump in 1990 was considered worthy of today's headline, right? Yes, if you were a chief purveyor of fake news and infectious carrier of TDS like Yahoo, Bing, Huffpost, etc. Apparently, if you believed these reports, Trump and Sinatra got into a dispute over the latter's appearance fee at the then new Trump Casino. When the renowned negotiator argued for a lower fee, Ol Blue Eyes purportedly said blank Donald Trump. The President had just announced historic legislation aimed at overhauling our outdated immigration system. Did that make the headlines? No, the Trump-haters in the media felt the ancient Sinatra snipe warranted more coverage.

Liberals everywhere led by their new vanguard; the violent, anarchistic fascists from Anti-Fa, staged demonstrations against Christopher Columbus on Columbus Day. They labeled Columbus a white supremacist and terrorist. These pied pipers of historical ignorance led their equally uninformed sheeple in denigrating the great explorer and humanitarian along with all Italian-Americans and the Latino people who owed their origin to Columbus.

This great lie had been foisted upon the American people by our failed, corrupt education (indoctrination) system and ideologically motivated media who were intent upon destroying our history, flag and every cherished symbol that held our people together. I implored everyone to please read *Uncle Sam's White Hat* to get a balanced view of American history. I felt it should be made required reading in our schools.

I remembered how Jemele Hill, one of ESPN's
left-wing political advocates had posed as a sports
pundit. ESPN had failed to take any meaningful
corrective action earlier when she called President
Trump a white supremacist surrounded by other white
supremacists. This time around she showed her
complete ignorance by calling for a boycott of the
Dallas Cowboys' sponsors in reaction to Jerry Jones'
announcement that his players would not be allowed
to play in games if they refused to stand for the
national anthem.

Was she really that dense to not realize that these
same sponsors contributed big, big bucks to ESPN?
Surely jeopardizing ESPN's bottom line this way
served as justifiable grounds for her termination,
right? No, instead she received a suspension. Curt
Schilling must have been scratching his head. Even
though her punishment fell far below the
consequences others had faced for lesser infractions,
the race baiters like Al Sharpton still had the nerve to
come out to defend her.

10/10/17: More women came out of the woodwork to
charge one of the most powerful men in Hollywood,

movie mogul Harvey Weinstein, with gross and widespread sexual harassment and three even accused him of rape. In what was apparently one of the worst kept secrets in Tinsel Town, Weinstein had purportedly subjected scads of women, including some of Hollywood's best known actresses, to sexual abuse for over twenty years.

According to reports, he had regularly exposed himself to women as part of his unwanted advances. The media that loved trashing President Trump and dishing dirt on conservatives remained relatively mute on Weinstein's exploits. Worse, high level Democrats including Hillary Clinton, Chuck Schumer and Nancy Pelosi remained mum even though they had received millions from the Hollywood heavyweight. Ho hum, hypocrisy and double standards remained par for the course among liberals.

10/11/17: Nick Dudich, the Audience Strategy Editor for NYT Video (How about that title!), was caught on hidden camera by Project Veritas bragging about slanting their coverage of Donald Trump. He called himself the "gatekeeper" for any video released online and crowed about making sure everything reflected his negative bias. Dudich enthusiastically admitted to doing everything possible to destroy the Trump "threat" including going after his children.

He outlined his strategy for forcing President Trump to resign; he sought to destroy his businesses and his children's businesses by calling for boycotts of their hotels, etc. Was there any wonder that Donald Trump had repeatedly referred to this rag as the failing NYT? This wasn't an idle claim but represented an actual fact. The NYT was failing financially because people were smarter than the NYT thought and could recognize fake news and biased coverage.

The U. S. Supreme Court dismissed the Maryland case against President Trump's travel ban. The vote was unanimous! After treating viewers to a barrage of negative coverage for many months, how did the media handle this gigantic win for the Trump Administration? Yep, they buried it or tried to downplay its significance by holding out hope that the court might take a different view of the Hawaii challenge ... pathetic!

Representatives for sexual sicko Harvey Weinstein announced that the movie mogul was headed to Europe for sexual rehabilitation therapy. Translation: he was taking off for Europe to escape the heat for a while. How long would it take for the media and liberal sycophants everywhere to sweep this scandal under the rug? Deplorables could only imagine what would have happened to a conservative exposed for the same transgressions.

NBC News reported that President Trump asked to have the U. S.' nuclear arsenal increased tenfold during a staff meeting. President Trump declared the story to be another example of fake news from NBC. NBC claimed to have three unnamed sources from within the meeting. Secretary of Defense James Mattis who attended the meeting also came out publicly and stated that the story was absolutely false.

The Boy Scouts of America announced that they would start accepting girls into the Cub Scouts and Boy Scouts. Holy moly, now we couldn't have separate clubs and organizations for boys??? Some claimed the move was financially motivated due to dropping membership. This may have been true since the Boy Scouts previously caved in to insane political correctness when they decided to allow homosexual Scout leaders in the organization; a move which surely thinned the ranks of the formerly traditional organization.

Personally, I thought the decision reflected today's mixed up politics but perhaps financial considerations did come into play. Maybe the Boy Scouts figured they could save money by utilizing same sex bathrooms. Deplorables wondered if they would change the organization's name to the Transgender Scouts of America. On a more serious note, Deplorables took this as another sign we were losing our culture and history right before our very eyes.

10/13/17: Less than a month earlier, MO State Rep. Maria Chappelle-Nadal had been let off the hook with a meaningless censure after posting online that she hoped President Trump would be assassinated. The "contrite Christian" showed her true colors by creating another disgusting online post. This time she juxtaposed pictures of President Trump and Adolph Hitler. If Governor Greitens had a spine, this time he would have followed through with what he should have done the first time by having her removed from the State House.

President Trump said he would issue an executive order ending subsidies to insurance companies. The Justice Department had ruled them illegal because the payments had not been authorized by an appropriation from Congress. This ruling didn't surprise anyone who had taken a junior high school civics course since only Congress and not the President controlled the purse strings of our government.

Nancy Pelosi came out immediately and said she hadn't read the executive order yet but knew it was an act of sabotage by the President against the American people. I thought we'd never see another gem like her famous quote on Obamacare that we had to pass the bill to see what was in the bill but she may have topped her own stupidity and audacity this time. Deplorables applauded President Trump for forcing the Congress to do their job. In so many words he told them to get off their duffs and pass legislation if they wanted to authorize what amounted to socialistic wealth redistribution.

10/14/17: Hillary Clinton made the news yet again by stating that America put a person who committed sexual assault in the White House. Even for her this remark seemed brazenly hypocritical while she ignored the growing claims of sexual assault and rape against her good friend of many years and staunch political supporter, Harvey Weinstein. At first, many people thought Mrs. Clinton was talking about her husband who had committed sexual harassment, assault and, according to some claims, rape while President. Certainly she didn't mean President Trump who was only guilty of gross locker room talk some twenty years prior. Deplorables pleaded again for Hillary to please go away, back into the woods!

10/16/17: A school district in Biloxi, MS banned Harper Lee's classic novel *To Kill a Mockingbird* in order to protect children from offensive language. This was in keeping with the fanatics who destroyed Confederate and other statues in an attempt to wipe out our history. *Mockingbird*, an absolute classic, spanned many decades as a clarion call for equal justice and civil rights. The monumental masterpiece did as much or more than any other work of art to change attitudes towards race in a positive way.

The novel was set in the Depression Era-South so naturally it used the setting's racially insensitive language and reflected the backward attitudes of that time and place. Liberal loon snowflakes wanted to eradicate it even though the uplifting tome exposed evil and concluded with justice prevailing. Liberals truly were mentally ill.

We hit a trifecta of finger pointing that served as a fitting tribute to our age of no personal accountability. Hillary Clinton came out with more Trump bashing and tried to re-litigate the 2016 election by blaming everyone but herself for her loss. No surprise there but on the same day, two other malcontents joined in on the blame game.

Colin Kaepernick filed a grievance against the NFL owners claiming collusion as the reason why he remained out of work. He felt it had nothing to do with his eroded skills or the horrible-for-business distraction he had created. Although it seemed impossible, Bowe Bergdahl topped Kaepernick and admitted guilt as a deserter but blamed President Trump for his inability to get a fair trial. We were supposed to forget about the six brave soldiers who later died searching for the deserter and enemy sympathizer.

Hillary couldn't resist taking advantage of the harmonic convergence of liberal finger pointing. She chimed in to support Kaepernick and claimed that his kneeling had nothing to do with the flag or anthem but instead represented a reverent act aimed at bringing attention to rampant oppression and social injustice. If it had nothing to do with the flag or anthem then why in the hell did Kaepernick decide to protest during the national anthem? Of course he was taking a cheap shot at our nation! Deplorables recalled how his socks depicted police officers as pigs.

Deplorables felt Kaepernick and company should have taken a knee for all of the police officers assassinated since BLM had declared war on cops including the most recent murder of a black police officer in New Orleans. They believed Kaepernick was complicit and guilty of inciting the kind of hatred and violence that led to murder.

Jimmy Kimmel stated during an interview that he didn't mind if Republicans didn't tune into his late night "comedy" show. He said that if they didn't agree with his political stands he didn't want to have a conversation with them anyway. Deplorables couldn't imagine Johnny Carson or Jay Leno telling half of their potential audience to get lost if they didn't agree with them politically. Even a far left loon like David Letterman knew better than to intentionally tell conservative viewers to kiss off. Deplorables thought Jimmy might want to try sticking to comedy.

10/17/17: President Trump held two press conferences after first meeting with his cabinet and later with Senate Majority Leader Mitch McConnell to discuss crucial issues facing the country and the Congress. What made the biggest news? Was it tax reform, health care, the Iran nuclear deal or North Korea? No, amidst all of these weighty topics the Press wanted to know whether President Trump called the parents of the four American servicemen killed in Niger.

The President responded that past Presidents including Obama hadn't called parents. It seemed clear he meant that they hadn't always called but sometimes wrote letters or contacted them in person. However, the Press put the worst construction on it and claimed he meant President Obama <u>never</u> called the parents of troops killed in battle. This created yet another tempest in a teapot that detracted from the important news the people needed to hear. And so it went.

10/18/17: FL Rep. Frederica Wilson (D) was riding in the car with the widow of slain U. S. Serviceman La David Johnson when President Trump called to offer his condolences. She purportedly heard part of the conversation on the speaker phone. She claimed President Trump heartlessly told the grieving widow that Johnson "knew what he signed up for but I guess it still hurts."

President Trump denied Wilson's claim and said he had proof of her lying. Even if he misspoke in this way, which was highly doubtful, why would a U. S. Representative make an issue out of it while supposedly comforting a grieving widow of one of our military heroes? The answer was simple: politics. Frederica Wilson, an unhinged liberal suffering from TDS, had called for the President's impeachment. This showed once again how liberals had taken politics way over the line of anything resembling decency.

10/19/17: ISIS had come to power under President Obama's watch. He had stood by and did nothing to halt their advance as they set up a caliphate stretching across parts of Iraq, Syria and elsewhere that provided a base of operations for worldwide terror strikes including against the U. S. The media had given him a pass for this stunning failure and hailed his "leadership" after he had mounted a counter-offensive that consisted of sporadic bombing runs that did nothing to uproot their evil. This went on for years and cost thousands of people their lives and freedom. It also resulted in refugee crises that had threatened to destroy Europe. At least the Brits said enough is enough and Brexited from the European Union.

When President Trump took office, he called our enemies by name, radical Islamic terrorists, and changed President Obama's rules of engagement that had handcuffed our military. He stated in no uncertain terms that our goal was to eradicate ISIS and their ilk. He made a trip to the Middle East and convened the leaders of some fifty nations to solicit their help and assured them we had their backs.

First the American-backed allies freed Mosul and then rooted out ISIS from their capital and stronghold in Raqqa, Syria after only nine months with President Trump in office. As of this writing, ISIS had lost eighty percent of the territory they'd gained for their caliphate under President Obama's feckless leadership. How did the mainstream media handle this absolutely incredible turnaround and stunning victory? Did they heap praise on the new Administration like they would have done without ceasing had it occurred under President Obama's watch?

You knew the answer. They kept ginning up silly, disgusting, politically polarizing controversies like the one involving Frederica Wilson's spurious claims about condolences offered to the family of La David Johnson and didn't mention Trump's rollback of ISIS. Oftentimes, the news the media didn't report was more damning than the lies they spread.

Chief of Staff, General John Kelly made a surprise visit to the rostrum of the White House Press

Briefing to explain the truth behind President Trump's condolences to the family of slain hero La David Johnson. Kelly, a gold star father himself, explained that he had advised President Trump to tell the family that David died doing what he wanted to do, that was, fighting for his country. He told the group of reporters how this had comforted him when General Dunford notified him of his Marine son's death in combat. In a wholly dignified way, General Kelly said he was stunned and heartbroken that a U. S. Congresswoman had used something so sacred to try to score political points.

Ignorant, self-serving, military-hating Frederica Wilson doubled down and said that General Kelly was only trying to save his job. Other despicable liberals came out to insult and castigate the honorable General. When advised of the White House's response by a member of the Press, Wilson laughed and said she was a "rock star." CNN commentator and former Hillary Clinton Aid, Brian Fallon, called the distinguished General Kelly "odious" and said people shouldn't be distracted by his uniform. Did Deplorables need more proof that liberalism was a mental illness?

Former President George W. Bush had spent eight long years listening to President Obama blame him for everything wrong with America. Even in the last year of his second term, President Obama had still refused to take responsibility for his own actions. Nevertheless, President Bush had refused to comment publicly about his successor, apparently wanting to maintain the dignity of the office.

Only nine short months into President Trump's first term, W. came out and criticized the President for his brash style. Although Deplorables loved the President's hard-hitting, forthright straight-talk and willingness to take on the liberals and establishment Republicans, President Bush felt the need to criticize him and, in effect, blamed President Trump for the divisiveness generated by lunatic liberals and their media enablers. Why would he do this? It was the same reason why John McCain refused to repeal and replace Obamacare as he'd promised to do: personal vendetta. Bush denigrated the office he once held in order to take a swipe at the man who had whipped his wimpy brother's butt in the 2016 GOP primary campaign. I had voted for him twice but had to admit that W. was nothing but a sore loser and coward.

10/21/17: MSNBC's unhinged left-wing cheerleader and TDS-sufferer, Rachel Maddow, concocted a wild conspiracy theory blaming President Trump's "Muslim Travel Ban" (her words) for the death of four American Green Berets in Niger. She theorized that Chad removed their troops from Niger due to the latest travel ban that included Chad and consequently their absence led to the ambush that killed our heroes.

There was just a small problem. Chad never claimed any connection between the travel restrictions and their troop movements. The geography alone would have dissuaded any sane person from making such a claim but Maddow didn't need any research or actual facts to propagate her hateful rhetoric. With such grievous bias and sloppy journalism, even some left-wing media sources denounced her including the Huffington Post. If there was a downpour after Rachel Maddow went through Blue Iguana, did she believe she had made it rain by washing her car???

10/22/17: Representative Maxine Waters (CA) must have grown envious of Frederica Wilson for stealing headlines and her thunder as the number one clown with a megaphone in the Democrat Party. She emerged from the sidelines to essentially threaten the President with assassination by publicly proclaiming she wanted to "take out" Donald Trump. Where was the Secret Service these days? Hello ... McFly ... wasn't it illegal to threaten the President? Or were Johnny Depp, Maria Chappelle-Nadal, Kathy Griffin and Maxine Waters above the law like Hillary?

10/24/17: Senator Jeff Flake (R, AZ) announced he would not seek re-election in 2018. He then proceeded to offer a sanctimonious lecture to President Trump. Hmmmm ... let's see ... what did Senator Flake have in common with Senator Bob Corker (R, TN) and Senator John McCain (R, AZ)?

All three had engaged in ugly vitriol while criticizing the President when he responded to critics by fighting fire with fire. These three hypocrites were all nothing but cowards. Flake and Corker had decided not to run for re-election and John McCain knew another run was highly unlikely due to his unfortunate health issues. So they took cheap shots at the President while running away from the challenge of facing the electorate, the American people.

All three were also RINOs who had no business calling themselves Republicans much less conservatives. They could rant, rave and throw tantrums all they wanted but Deplorables saw this for what it was. This was called draining the swamp. Yes, some of the worst denizens of the swamp in D. C. were Republicans.

10/26/17: In the latest installment of truth is stranger than fiction, a boomerang thrown by Democrats a year ago had come back around to smack them in the face. Cries of Russian collusion echoed hollowly for month after month because, despite two endless and expensive congressional investigations and another one led by Robert Mueller and his pack of Hillary donors, no one could produce any legitimate evidence of collusion on the part of Donald Trump or his campaign because … drum roll … it was a hoax. It never happened outside of the contrived accusations leveled by the fake news media.

However, it finally came to light that the fabricated Trump Dossier concocted by Fusion GPS with the help of a British spy and Russian backers was financed by Hillary Clinton's campaign and led by the

Podesta brothers and the DNC. An even more astounding revelation came to light. The FBI, under Robert Mueller at the time, knew in advance that the Russians tried to corner the market on U. S. Uranium through influence peddling that apparently benefitted Bill Clinton ($500 thousand speech fee) and the Clinton Foundation (perhaps $135 million). Yet, the State Department and other agencies approved the Uranium One deal that put twenty percent of our nation's uranium in Russian hands.

Mueller kept quiet and let the Clintons and the Obama Administration jeopardize our national security, apparently for Putin payola. The hypocrisy and irony were too overwhelming for words. Robert Mueller, the guy trying to pin collusion on President Trump without a shred of evidence, apparently aided and abetted the Clintons and Obama Administration in colluding with Russia to not only influence our elections (fake dossier) but weaken our national security (Uranium One).

Was there a stronger word than brazen? The Russians contributed most of the tainted millions to the Canadian branch of the Clinton Foundation to apparently skirt U. S. reporting laws. An FBI undercover informant who had the dirt on all of this several years ago was silenced by the Obama Justice Department through a non-disclosure agreement (NDA) and subsequent threats. AG Jeff Sessions lifted the gag order on this whistle blower and Democrats scurried for cover in anticipation of his testimony. What was that old saying? Oh yeah, people in glass houses shouldn't throw stones ... or boomerangs.

10/31/17: NYC suffered another Jihadist terrorist attack at the hands of Sayfullo Saipov who rented a truck from Home Depot to mow down eight people and injure at least eleven others in Manhattan not far from the site of the 9/11 attack on the World Trade Center. The twenty-nine-year-old Muslim pledged allegiance to ISIS. After running over the innocent pedestrians and bicyclers, he purposefully crashed his truck into a school bus carrying small children before exiting and praising his false god Allah while attempting suicide via police shooting.

Saipov was shot but survived. While recovering in the hospital, reporters said he appeared gleeful about his successful attack. He had entered the U. S. legally

… get this … as part of our Diversity Visa Program. Yes, you heard that right. To the surprise of many, we'd been running an immigration lottery to bring fifty-thousand refugees into our country to promote diversity from underrepresented nations of the world. This insane program was the brainchild of none other than Senate Minority Leader Chuck Schumer. It wasn't enough for "Crying" Chuck that America was already the most diverse nation on earth. Apparently, he felt our diversity needed to include more Muslim terrorists.

Amazingly, none of the Democrats came out to call for more gun control. Oh yeah, he used a truck. Pictures quickly surfaced since Saipov had a mug shot on file from a previous arrest. I hated to say it but the heavily bearded Saipov looked like a stereotypical Jihadi. Within hours, the authorities revealed that his mosque had been under surveillance for years. Someone also produced a photo from back in August where ISIS had posted a picture of the crime-scene-to-be. Somehow, our politically correct security apparatus failed to pick up on these obvious signs.

It was no wonder since NY was run by two of the most wild-eyed liberals around. NY Governor Andrew Cuomo and NYC Mayor Bill De Blasio held a press conference and issued this confidence builder (I'm paraphrasing to save space and cut through all the spin.). They basically said this was the new normal so New Yorkers should get used to it.

Saipov came from Uzbekistan, a country not named in the travel ban yet it seemed horribly ironic that Hawaiian Activist Judge Derrick Watson had recently struck down President Trump's third version of the travel ban aimed at protecting Americans from such terrorists. Watson didn't seem at all bothered by having more blood on his hands. In another bit of horrible irony, the victims included five Argentinians and one German. I bet this did wonders for tourism in the Big Apple.

To add icing to this putrid cake … or caramel on top of the sour Big Apple … reporters interviewed acquaintances who said he was a normal, nice guy. The fact that Saipov had a wife and small children at home showed the fanaticism and utter disregard for humanity of radical Islamic terrorists. Would this lead to a bi-partisan effort to jettison the Diversity Visa Program and shore up our leaky immigration system? Deplorables everywhere held our collective breath ... NOT!

11/3/17: Snoop Dogg posted a cover photo on Instagram promoting his album. It featured him standing over a flag draped corpse with a "Trump" toe tag. The caption read "Make America Crip Again." This followed his earlier photo where he appeared to shoot a likeness of President Trump in clown makeup. It was bad enough that he proudly trumpeted his affiliation with the notorious Crips gang that had been responsible for so many murders. But Deplorables were left wondering again if the U. S. Justice Department and Secret Service maintained a double standard toward Donald Trump when it came to enforcing laws that prohibited making threats against the President. Apparently, the law didn't apply to Snoop Dogg, Kathy Griffin, Maxine Waters, Maria Nadal-Chappelle, Johnny Depp and others of their ilk.

Colonel Jeffrey R. Nance concluded the sentencing phase of Sergeant Bowe Bergdahl's military tribunal for desertion and misbehavior before the enemy, behavior that endangered and cost the lives of American troops. Astonishingly, Nance did not punish Bergdahl with any prison time. President Trump rightly called the decision a disgrace.

In 2009 Bergdahl left his post and wandered off the base to consort with the enemy and six brave soldiers were wounded in the search for the deserter. Sergeant Mark Allen was shot in the head and lost the ability to walk and talk. This disgusting display of outrageous injustice shined more light on the corruption within our Justice System, civilian and military, where the just were punished and criminals were feted as heroes.

President Obama had freed five of the worst Muslim terrorists at Guantanamo in order to barter for Bergdahl's release. All five Jihadists had returned to the battlefield to kill American troops. President Obama had welcomed the deserter home to a ceremony in the Rose Garden along with his parents and hailed him as a hero. Bergdahl should have at least received a life sentence. In the not too distant past, he would have swiftly been shot by a firing squad as a traitor. Deplorables thought Colonel Nance should be court martialed.

11/4/17: A reporter for the L. A. Times, who will remain unnamed since I don't want to give him any notoriety, insulted Sarah Huckabee Sanders. He called her a chunky soccer mom who, because of her appearance, was not fit to be the President's Press Secretary. He offered a perfunctory apology shortly thereafter but the mainstream media still let him off the hook rather easily. In the age of identity politics when conservatives were often gleefully labeled as sexist or misogynistic, liberals proudly displayed their double standard through muted or non-existent criticism.

President Bill Clinton, the accused prolific sexual harasser and rapist, was still lovingly approved by the Left for his boys-will-be-boys, reprehensibly ribald behavior. Even serial harasser and rapist Harvey Weinstein continued to get a pass from some of his victims because of his Hollywood ties. Where were all of the feminists now? Why weren't they rushing to the defense of Sarah Sanders? The answer was simple.

They were hypocrites who gave priority to their evil ideology over decency.

George H. W. Bush and George W. Bush made some incredibly derogatory remarks about President Trump in a newly released book that I will leave unnamed so as to not promote it. Among other insults, they labeled President Trump a "blowhard." The elder Bush even said he didn't vote for Trump in 2016. George W. Bush had gone out of his way to never criticize President Barack Obama even though Obama had made a habit of blaming his predecessor for all of his own failures. W. had claimed he didn't want to speak out since it might denigrate the office of the presidency.

How about Bush Senior voting for Hillary? I guessed we should thank the old codger for showing unequivocally that the D. C. establishment was comprised of RINO Republicans as well as Democrats. They had all contracted TDS and couldn't stand the President since he was an outsider determined to shake up the status quo. It drove them insane to think they might lose their grip on the thing that was most precious to them: not the good of the

American people but their own power and influence. Deplorables challenged President Trump to do what we elected him to do ... drain the Swamp!

Senator Rand Paul was attacked by his neighbor while mowing his lawn at his Kentucky home. Apparently motivated by his liberal politics, the enraged neighbor pummeled Paul so severely that it left him with five broken ribs and a bruised lung. The attacker was only charged with fourth degree assault, a misdemeanor. Why wasn't he charged with felony battery or even attempted murder? If politically motivated as it appeared, shouldn't this have been a so called hate crime?

Apparently, it was open season on conservatives as evidenced by Rep. Steve Scalise, the country music fans in Las Vegas and President Trump who had received multiple death threats that went unpunished. When Anti-Fa attacked conservatives with clubs, they were labeled as cuddly counter-protesters.

11/5/17: The Anti-Justice Department seemed a more fitting name for our Justice Department. Activist judges were regularly allowed to obstruct the

President in carrying out his duties according to his clearly codified constitutional powers. More than a year had passed and no evidence of Russian collusion had been unearthed despite millions of taxpayer dollars being wasted. Yet, clear evidence of influence peddling on the part of the Clinton campaign continued to be swept under the rug.

A close aide of John McCain resisted a subpoena related to the fake Fusion GPS dossier. What did he have to hide? Did McCain collude with the Clintons and DNC in trying to smear candidate Trump? The topper was Bowe Bergdahl. Not only did he get off scot free but now his lawyer was calling for the deserter to receive a medal for his valor as a prisoner of war. He wasn't a POW ... he voluntarily left his post and sought out the enemy!

Another mass shooting occurred, this time in a small Baptist Church in tiny Sutherland Springs, TX with a population of less than five-hundred. The killer murdered twenty-six people, some at point blank range in execution style and wounded at least twenty others. The victims included small children, senior citizens, the pastor's daughter and a pregnant woman and her eight-month-old baby in the womb. Democrats predictably jumped in immediately to politicize the tragedy by calling for gun control. One zombie-like liberal reporter from NBC (National Bureau of Communists?) even asked President Trump a question about gun control during his press conference with South Korea's President during his critical Asia-Pacific trip.

This line of questioning was rendered even more inappropriate by the news that the shooter had been jailed for a year while in the Air Force for assaulting his wife and cracking the skull of his infant stepson. The Air Force failed to report the crime to the Feds. If they would have done so, the shooter would not have been able to pass the background check that allowed him to purchase the guns used in the mass murder. Hey folks, we had plenty of gun laws on the books! We just needed to enforce them. This example provided more proof on top of the mountain of evidence already in existence that we simply couldn't trust the government to protect us.

In another bit of bitter irony, one of the two heroes who confronted the deranged gunman and saved numerous lives, Stephen Willeford, turned out to be a NRA member and past NRA instructor. As the media made hay out of our latest tragedy, I couldn't help but wonder about the fecklessness of our government and justice system. In almost every case it seemed like the killers were on somebody's radar screen but no action was taken.

11/6/17: Actor Michael McKean of Lenny and Squiggy fame reached a new low even for Hollywood liberals. When House Speaker Paul Ryan asked for prayers for the victims of the mass shooting in Sutherland Springs, TX, McKean responded, "They were in church. They had the prayers shot right out of them. Maybe try something else."

In the midst of an historic Asia-Pacific trip with the President addressing such weighty matters as averting a nuclear war with North Korea and erasing our enormous trade imbalance with China, the media decided another issue warranted greater coverage. They criticized President Trump for dumping his entire small box of fish meal into a coy carp pond. Even in the midst of such TDS insanity, the media also proved to be incredibly disingenuous. During the video coverage they showed over and over, they failed to mention that President Trump only followed suit after Japanese Prime Minister Shinzo Abe dumped the entire contents of his box to the delight of the hungry fish.

11/7/17: While riding her bike, Juli Briskman of Virginia flipped off the President as his motorcade passed by. While rude, offensive and immature for a fifty-year-old woman, she had every right to express her First Amendment Rights in this ill-advised manner. However, she went further and posted a picture of her vulgar act on social media. This prompted her employer, a government contractor called Akima LLC, to terminate her for violating the company's code of conduct that prohibited lewd or obscene posts on social media. Showing just how delusional and insane liberals were who had been infected with TDS, she contacted the ACLU to sue her employer and stated she would do the same thing if given the chance again.

More news leaked out to bring James Comey's credibility and character into question. An early draft of the former FBI Director's memo concerning Hillary

Clinton's email scandal used the term "gross negligence" to describe her behavior. Then it somehow changed to "extreme carelessness" in the final draft. This proved to be consistent with former AG Loretta Lynch's instruction to Comey to refer to the Clinton probe as a "matter" rather than an investigation.

It didn't take a genius to figure out the motivation. Gross negligence was a statutory term punishable as a criminal offense. Where in the hell was AG Jeff Sessions? Robert Mueller continued to indict people like Paul Manafort for alleged crimes that had nothing to do with collusion between the Trump campaign and Russia while the entire Justice Department turned a blind eye to a treasure trove of evidence that should have easily led to indictments of the Clintons and others including Loretta Lynch and possibly Barack Obama. The evidence also pointed to Special Counsel Robert Mueller who headed the FBI during some of the apparent crimes that were overlooked.

Rather than denouncing Michael McKean's detestable comments about prayer, the mainstream media piled on. CNN and other outlets jumped in to denounce prayer and mock God. This revealed something important about the political divide in America. It was no longer about Democrats versus Republicans or liberals against conservatives. When you pulled back the covers, it really came down to a battle between good and evil. Progressive secular humanists were against life, family, marriage, Christian morals and basically any public display of faith. In short, they were opposed to God, His people and His teachings.

11/10/17: As the Republicans pushed to pass tax reform through the Congress before year's end, the media threw a curveball with stories of allegations of sexual abuse against Alabama's GOP senatorial candidate, Roy Moore. The accusations stemmed from previously unfiled claims that allegedly occurred several decades before but no one questioned the authenticity of the allegations. No one seemed curious as to why the accusers remained silent for so long and waited for the most opportune time to derail Moore's Senate run and the GOP's chances of passing the tax cut. Was it just an incredible consequence?

Under normal circumstances, people would wait patiently in a country where the accused were supposedly innocent until proven guilty but not in our highly politicized, divided nation. The most despicable offenders again proved to be members of the Republican establishment who immediately called for Moore to withdraw before getting his day in court even though Moore declared the accusations to be completely false.

11/12/17: Former CIA Director John Brennan and Former Director of National Intelligence James Clapper made a splash with the mainstream media by chastising President Trump for stating that Vladimir Putin believed his claim that Russia had not tried to interfere in our 2016 election. They offered all kinds of hypothetical motivations as if they could read the President's mind or had PhDs in psychology. They failed to note that the President didn't say he believed Putin. Of course they didn't mention how Hillary Clinton colluded with the Russians while accepting huge bribes through the Clinton Foundation (aka money laundering operation). Apparently, they also forgot how President Obama, unaware of the hot microphone, had told Russian President Dmitri

Medvedev to advise Vladimir Putin that he would have "more flexibility" to negotiate with Putin after the 2012 election.

President Trump referred to Brennan, Clapper and former FBI Director James Comey as political hacks. President Trump hit the nail on the head. Never in the history of our nation had leaders of our intelligence and law enforcement agencies been so politically motivated and biased. In my opinion, the President was much too kind. He could have labeled them as treasonous criminals who had completely eroded the citizenry's trust in the impartiality of federal agencies tasked with blindly following the rule of law for every American regardless of ideology or party affiliations. Thanks to the Obama Administration's willingness to use federal bureaucratic power in the Justice Department, IRS and other agencies to pursue political aims, Lady Justice had been forced to shed her blindfold. Conservatives and Christians needed to beware!

11/13/17: The liberal media provided some comic relief in the ongoing tar and feathering of Judge Roy Moore. They turned to none other than Groping Joe

Biden for moral clarity on the Judge's alleged indiscretions. Other than Bill Clinton was there a higher ranking Democrat more celebrated than Joe Biden for being prolific at making women feel uncomfortable with his inappropriate touching, humiliating comments and innuendo?

Moore's fate looked more tenuous every day as new allegations surfaced and establishment Republicans rushed to throw him under the bus. Perhaps Judge Moore was a bad egg but nothing had been proven yet. Had we forgotten Al Sharpton's Tawana Brawley rape hoax or the Duke Lacrosse rush to judgment that had ruined several innocent young men's lives through false pretenses?

Whether Roy Moore was proven guilty or not, two questions needed to be raised. Why was there such a double standard? There was one set of rules and punishments for conservatives and another for liberals. Bill Clinton received a wink and a nod and even admiration in some circles while Hillary and the media shamed his female accusers with merciless scorn. Why was there such a rush to judgment? Men were regularly convicted immediately in the court of public opinion with help from the media any time a woman raised an accusation, no matter how many decades had passed and whether any credible evidence was provided beyond he-said-she-said here-say.

11/14/17: In comic relief part two, several Democrats on the Hill brought forth articles of impeachment against President Trump. Here was one example of the terrible transgressions they cited. According to Rep. Steve Cohen (D, TN) and several of his other loony tune colleagues suffering from TDS, President Trump violated the Constitution's Emoluments Clause which prohibited the receipt of gifts and favors from foreign states. How did President Trump fall under the influence of corrupt foreigners? The President was a shareholder in the Trump business empire that included a hotel in Washington, D. C.

Believe it or not, visitors from foreign states sometimes booked rooms in this hotel when they traveled to our nation's capital. Thus, when they paid their hotel bill, the President was notified immediately that a few hundred dollars had hit the billionaire's coffers and he rushed to return the favor. Deplorables thanked loony liberals for giving us a great laugh. It was too bad that these same folks didn't see anything wrong with Hillary Clinton and the rest of the Obama Administration allowing Russia to heist twenty percent of our uranium in a pay-for-play deal that netted $140 million for the Clinton Foundation.

GQ Magazine named Colin Kaepernick as their man of the year. What did he do to deserve this dubious distinction? Deplorables recalled his exploits back to the beginning. He had initiated the disrespectful practice of protesting by kneeling during the national anthem before NFL games. As a San Francisco 49er and elitist one-percenter making millions of dollars per year, he had claimed to be oppressed. He hadn't hidden the fact that he chose to use the anthem and flag as his platform because of his dislike of the United States and law enforcement.

If anyone had any doubts about his motives, he had made his sentiments perfectly clear by wearing socks depicting police officers as pigs and a t-shirt hailing murderous terrorist Che Guevara as a hero. He had lost his job by letting his quarterback skills decline while shifting his focus to promoting ill-defined social causes. Kaepernick had become such a liability and distraction that no other NFL team would touch him with a ten-foot pole.

He had shown his total lack of character by stating he would stand for the anthem if another NFL team would pick him up. When that didn't work, he had filed a grievance against the NFL for collusion even though he had no one to blame for his predicament but himself. He had inspired other "oppressed" millionaires to take up the fight for him. In the process, Kaepernick and his fellow protesters had alienated many NFL fans and caused attendance and viewership to drop dramatically. Kaepernick had led the way in ruining one of America's great past-times and causing further divisions in our already woefully divided nation. That was your man of the year; hail Kaepernick! Thankfully, hardly anyone read GQ and now no sane person would ever take them seriously.

11/15/17: A trio of UCLA basketball players on tour in China got caught stealing some very expensive sunglasses. They could have been imprisoned for multiple years under Chinese law. Their boneheaded move seemed inexplicably foolish considering what had happened to Otto Warmbier for a lesser infraction in North Korea. Warmbier had suffered terrible torture that left him a vegetable and resulted in his death shortly after being released and returned to the United States. He had languished in North Korea for years while the Obama Administration twiddled their thumbs.

President Trump took immediate action and convinced Chinese President Xi to release the three young men back to the United States. Did the Press laud President Trump for using his influence to help the young black men? Did they tone down their racial rhetoric toward the President and give him an atta boy? Nope ... they used the occasion of his post-trip press conference to criticize him for taking a drink of water during his speech. Deplorables stopped and pondered in amazement. After seventeen days on an historic trip punctuated by numerous significant accomplishments; after a long, grueling flight, they begrudged him taking a swig from a bottle of water. If President Trump cured cancer, the TDS-infected media would criticize him for not eliminating heart disease too.

11/16/17: Deplorables thought liberals might benefit from reading the Bible once in a while. Senator Al Franken (D, MN) missed the part where Jesus told the angry mob that wanted to execute an adulteress that he who was without sin should cast the first stone. The joke was on the comedian turned Senator when radio hostess Leeann Tweeden accused him of sexual molestation when they appeared together as part of a USO show. She explained how he forced her to kiss him and then plunged his tongue into her mouth. Then she produced a photograph of their plane ride home where Franken mugged for the camera as he groped the sleeping woman's breasts. Caught red handed, Franken admitted guilt and offered an apology.

What happened next shined a bright light on the audacious hypocrisy of liberals, Democrats and establishment Republicans. They called for a Senate investigation. Were they kidding us? Just days before, without any such irrefutable evidence and in spite of his claims of innocence, everyone piled on to call for Judge Roy Moore's removal from the Alabama race for the U. S. Senate. Now with photographic evidence and an admission of guilt from Franken, the same lynch mob called for an investigation. What was there to investigate? He admitted it! There was a picture of him smiling while sexually assaulting a sleeping woman! The difference was that Franken was a godless liberal and Moore was a conservative Christian. Republican cowardice proved simply amazing once again … disgusting!

I supposed this could be considered more comic relief if we wanted to include gallows humor. Rosie O'Donnell attacked House Majority Whip Steve Scalise … yes, the one that barely survived being shot by a politically motivated left-wing loon … and called him an expletive for leading the charge to cut our taxes. She trotted out the same tired nonsense that the GOP wanted to rob the poor to give the rich a tax cut. It appeared she had no idea of the actual policy changes in the bill but instead relied on fake news talking points. Deplorables had some advice for Rosie: the best way to hide ignorance was to keep one's mouth shut.

On the same day, normally reserved Senator Orrin Hatch blew a gasket when one of his Democrat Senate colleagues spewed the same tired lies about tax cuts benefitting the rich at the expense of the poor. I found it rather gratifying to see the staid, old gentleman pitch a fit at the Democrat as he tried to use identity politics to incite class warfare.

More high comedy ensued, this time in the form of a farce. None other than Hillary Clinton performed before the cameras and the fawning liberal media yet again by stating that assigning a special prosecutor to investigate her misdeeds would be an abuse of power and violation of the Constitution. Deplorables laughed so hard they cried. Who wrote this stuff? With the irony so thick, it prompted a rumor that Hillary wanted to be cast in the lead role of a remake of the classic 1950s horror flick, *The Thing that Wouldn't Die*.

11/17/17: Deplorables loved it when brazen hypocrisy was exposed. It seemed like a regular occurrence these days. The latest stranger-than-fiction moment came when the Congressional Hispanic Caucus denied membership to U. S. Representative Carlos Carbelo. Why would the Caucus deny the request of a fellow Hispanic Congressman from Florida? Here was our first clue. Carbelo was a Republican. So we had to conclude that you could only be Hispanic if you agreed with the Democrats' left-wing ideology. If you were a conservative, your DNA had been zapped by your politics and you had been magically, genetically transformed from Hispanic to white.

What did this say for liberals clamoring for tolerance, diversity and inclusiveness? At least the liberals were consistent in applying their insane standards for ethnicity. Black conservatives weren't black and female conservatives weren't women. I didn't get the logic but, I guessed, it made perfect sense if Bruce Jenner could be named female of the year and men could use a restroom full of little girls if they happened to feel feminine at the time.

11/18/17: I thought the worst case of TDS occurred when the widow of the slain serviceman whom President Trump called to console let Rep. Frederica Wilson convince her that the President somehow intended to insult her. However, LaVar Ball, the father of one of the three UCLA basketball players detained in China for shoplifting somehow found a way to top the crazy cowboy hat lady.

Even though the President expended precious political capital with Chinese President Xi and prevented a long jail term or worse as in the case of Otto Warmbier, the wayward young man's father went public in declaring that President Trump hadn't really done anything of significance. He rationalized that President Trump just happened to be in China anyway and dismissed the shoplifting of ultra-expensive designer sunglasses while on potentially hostile foreign soil as no big deal. Deplorables thought this guy needed to meet with Otto Warmbier's parents. Maybe then he would get down on his knees to thank God for the President's willingness to go to bat for his son.

11/19/17: Amidst falling revenues, ratings and attendance, the NFL tried to boost their fortunes by going to Mexico City to play a game between the Raiders and Patriots. Oakland running back Marshawn Lynch sat on his butt on foreign soil when they played our national anthem. Could there be anything worse?

Yes, that despicable millionaire took things to a level below rock bottom when he stood for Mexico's national anthem. President Trump rightly and bravely called for his suspension and, of course, received a chorus of criticism from the lamestream media. Deplorables thought Marshawn should forfeit his U. S. citizenship and move to Mexico. As for the NFL, did those bozos really think their future rested in soccer crazy Mexico? Deplorables thought the NFL might want to cater to their core fans who wanted to see football … not ridiculous political folly during our national anthem.

Authorities in Pennsylvania searched for Rahmael Sal Holt who shot and killed twenty-five-year-old Police Officer Brian Shaw during a routine traffic stop. In Baltimore, a manhunt continued for the killer of black Officer Sean Suiter, an eighteen-year veteran, husband and father of five. The murderer shot Suiter in the head while he followed up on a homicide investigation.

Agent Rogelio Martinez died as a result of a traumatic head injury while patrolling our border with Mexico in Texas. His partner also suffered head trauma but survived in critical condition. (Later these injuries were cryptically attributed to their vehicle possibly being side swiped. By whom and for what reason remained a mystery.) These killings put three more exclamation points on the evil insanity espoused by thugs like Colin Kaepernick who had launched a war on law enforcement. It also helped to echo cries from Deplorables everywhere to "Build that wall!"

11/24/17: CNN Analyst and White House Press Room denizen April Ryan served up a sour, spoiled dish for the Thanksgiving holiday when she accused WH Press Secretary Sarah Huckabee Sanders of lying about her chocolate pecan pie. Briefly away from the normal grind, Sanders had offered some lighthearted fare by posting a picture of a pecan pie on social media while expressing her pleasure over the now rare opportunity to get into the kitchen. Hateful and hyper-partisan Ryan refused to take a day off from her usual vindictiveness toward the White House and demanded a picture of the actual pie on Ms. Sanders' table.

Sanders again tried to make light of the situation by saying she would bake and bring one of her special pies to Ryan. Ryan rebuffed her further by saying she'd have to actually witness the Press Secretary baking the pie but would refuse to eat any because she didn't trust her. April Ryan demonstrated her extreme bias in the Press Room daily but this went much further in showing how badly she was suffering from TDS. With everything going on in the world did we really need Pie-gate?

11/27/17: While President Trump presented an award to some Native American WWII veterans, he took the opportunity to call out Senator Elizabeth Warren by referring to her as Pocahontas. This sent the liberals into a tizzy. The frenzied media cabal lit into Sarah Huckabee Sanders at the WH Press Conference, indignantly questioning why the President used a racial slur while honoring Navajo Code Talkers. When she refused to take the race card bait, they feverishly asked whether the White House considered the comment offensive.

Sanders promptly put them in their place by saying Warren's false appropriation of Native American ancestry to further her career was what they should find as offensive. As usual, they turned a blind eye to the truth that Elizabeth "Pocahontas" Warren had falsely claimed to be part Cherokee in order to secure a high paying job as a Harvard Law Professor and make a successful Senate run in Massachusetts.

Deplorables got a good laugh when ABC News joined the lynch mob. Someone should have reminded them that their sister company, Disney, made millions off of the *Pocahontas* movie franchise. If referring to Pocahontas was racially insulting, then shouldn't they have stopped profiting off of such offensive material in their movies and merchandising?

President Trump appointed White House Budget Director Mick Mulvaney to a second post as Acting Director of the Consumer Financial Protection Bureau (CFPB). The outgoing Director, Richard Cordray, made his own appointment of his Deputy, Leandra English, to run the CFPB until President Trump got a permanent selection through Senate confirmation. This led to a leadership tussle that wound up in court. This was how far the opposition to President Trump had gone.

We were supposed to forget the constitutional powers of the President. According to loony Never-Trumpers, some outgoing, unelected bureaucrat at a bloated, meaningless agency had more authority than the President. Mick Mulvaney had unearthed the real issue months prior when he referred to the CFPB as a joke. Although the name sounded like a good thing for consumers, in truth the CFPB represented another layer of bloated bureaucracy created by President Obama to further strangle legitimate businesses.

Asked if he still felt the same way, Mulvaney bravely said yes and added that people would be frightened if they understood the kind of power he now had as Director of the CFPB to destroy lives and businesses with virtually no congressional oversight. Deplorables offered hallelujahs to President Trump for sticking to his guns by trying to limit the power, scope and waste of government.

11/28/17: President Trump continued his herculean efforts to prod Congress toward a tax cut for the American people by visiting Capitol Hill and offering to meet with the "Big Four" of Mitch McConnell, Paul Ryan, Chuck Schumer and Nancy Pelosi. As the President's limo arrived, Schumer stayed in the Senate chambers and grandstanded with a speech announcing his and Pelosi's refusal to meet with the President. Exhibiting unbelievably hypocritical hutzpah even for him, the Senate Minority Leader accused the President and Republicans of being unwilling to pursue a bi-partisan solution. Yes, we heard that right. While pulling a last-minute grandstanding stunt by backing out of his planned meeting with the President, Schumer argued that the President wasn't interested in bi-partisanship. TDS made "Crying" Chuck look coo-coo.

11/29/17: In what had become a daily dosage of "shocking news", Matt Lauer became the latest high profile male to suffer the wrath of out-of-control, female vigilantism. NBC immediately fired the longtime *Today* host after, they said, receiving one accusation of sexual misconduct from a female colleague. I was no fan of the liberal standard bearer and Clinton/Obama water carrier. Perhaps he was guilty or perhaps not but he received no due process.

Just one day prior, a wild-eyed female activist on Fox News said it all when she stated that if a few innocent men got hurt in the process, so be it. That's the mentality men faced. It was payback time. We were all guilty and there was no statute of limitations even if the supposed infraction occurred decades ago under very different, now unrecognizable social standards. Thanks to Dem political tactics, young women had bought into the notion of a war on women all because people didn't want to foot the bill for their free contraceptives.

What we had now was truly a **war on men**. If any woman accused a man of anything, he was immediately guilty and paid a hefty price by having a career ended and life ruined. The thing-that-wouldn't-die, Hillary Clinton, resurfaced quickly to claim this as evidence that all men, even liberals like Lauer and Charlie Rose, conspired to stop her election on the grounds of gender bias. Of course, it had to be true because Lauer once had the nerve to momentarily break from the liberal media's coddling of Hillary during her 2016 campaign to ask one semi-tough question about her email scandal.

11/30/17: **I marked this day as one where the tide shifted dramatically in favor of Deplorables**. A jury in San Francisco rendered not guilty verdicts against Jose Inez Garcia Zarate for murder, involuntary manslaughter and assault with a deadly weapon. They convicted him on a charge of being a felon in possession of a firearm. The acquittal shocked sane people everywhere as perhaps the most perverse miscarriage of justice in American history. At least O. J. Simpson claimed innocence and disingenuously vowed to find his wife's killer. No one disputed that Zarate held the gun that killed Kate Steinle in the prime of life. However, the jury bought into the nonsense that the gun fired by itself even though Zarate first claimed he intended to shoot at some seals and witnesses saw him throw the gun into the Bay before running away.

This case paralleled the O. J. Simpson trial in an important way. In both cases the defense turned the trials into referendums on social/political issues of the day. For O. J's attorneys, they played the race card. In this instance, they put President Trump's immigration policy on trial. Of course, this didn't play well in San Francisco, one of the nation's epicenters of open borders and lawlessness cloaked in sanctuary status.

One of Zarate's defense lawyer's offered this political spin, "From day one, this case was used as a means to foment hate, to foment division and to foment a program of mass deportation." After the verdict, one of Zarate's other lawyers, Matt Gonzalez, lectured President Trump by name, warning him not to disparage the verdict because, as someone under investigation by Special Counsel Mueller, he should appreciate due process, the presumption of innocence and the standard of reasonable doubt.

Here's what Deplorables took from this sickening display of Left Coast lunacy. Liberal Democrats like Nancy Pelosi and every other politician in San Francisco ascribed greater rights to illegal immigrants than American citizens. They could literally get away with murder as long as they provided a strong, new voting block for Democrats. Deplorables wanted justice. Deplorables wanted President Trump to BUILD THAT WALL!

12/1/17: They couldn't find anything else to complain about so the loony libs criticized First Lady Melania Trump for her exquisite White House Christmas decorations. I guessed TDS extended to the whole family, including Baron. Maybe the press just remained ticked off at the way President Trump put "Merry Christmas" back on the White House Christmas cards ... ho, ho, ho!

Did anyone doubt that the media was completely biased? If you fell into this category, your mind surely changed on this day ... unless you suffered from the mental illness known as liberalism. When former NSA Director Michael Flynn pleaded guilty to lying to the FBI, the media celebrated like the ball had just dropped in Times Square on New Year's Eve. Perhaps the worst exhibition came from *The View's* Joy Behar who erupted with exultation. ABC proclaimed that General Flynn had effectively delivered up President Trump on a silver platter of Russian collusion.

Brian Ross falsely reported that an informant told him Flynn confessed that then candidate Donald Trump had instructed him to contact Russian officials. The stock market reacted to this fake news by plummeting some four-hundred points. ABC later had to walk back their wishful thinking. Blinded by TDS, the frothing media forgot that Flynn served much longer in the Obama Administration than the twenty-five days he served under President Trump until being forced to resign for lying to Vice President Mike Pence. No one seemed to care about Flynn's many years of faithful service to our country including five in combat. The hoopla finally died down when it dawned on people that Flynn had already been outed for lying to the Vice President, a more egregious transgression than lying to the FBI.

If the truth be told, Special Counsel Robert Mueller employed draconian tactics in coercing Flynn to throw in the towel. Faced with years of expensive litigation and financial ruin, Flynn had no other choice. The next day, ABC announced they'd suspended Brian Ross for four weeks without pay for perpetuating a lie without proper journalistic vetting. We knew it was bad when ABC, the network that hated Donald Trump from top to bottom and spent every day trying to undermine his presidency, had to admit to fake news and publicly punish one of its "journalists."

12/2/17: Robert Mueller removed FBI Agent Peter Strzok from the investigation into Russian collusion and reassigned him to the HR department. Strzok previously worked on the investigation into Hillary Clinton's email scandal. In a case of investigators investigating investigators, the Justice Department revealed that Strzok had sent anti-Trump and pro-Hillary texts during the 2016 campaign. This shed some light on the real collusion during the 2016 presidential campaign, the Deep State's politicization of the FBI and rigged outcome of the Hillary email investigation.

Apparently, Mueller had to take action to try to cover his own tracks. It seemed Loretta Lynch, Mueller, Comey and agents in charge of the investigation into Hillary's gross negligence in handling top secret information relevant to our national security thought they could cover up the truth since, at the time; they felt Hillary was sure to win the election. When that didn't happen, they had to gin up the utter nonsense of collusion between Russia and the Trump campaign to divert attention away from their own crimes. It was time to turn the spotlights on not only Hillary but also Lynch, Bill Clinton, Mueller, Rosenstein, Comey and other participants in the Deep State's Watergate-on-steroids. Deplorables wondered if it reached all the way to the top.

12/4/17: The U. S. Supreme Court ruled in favor of the Trump Administration in allowing President Trump's travel ban to go into effect. They overrode the activist judges in the lower courts that issued injunctions against the bans. They also ruled that, even if the appeals under consideration in courts in San Francisco and Richmond, VA went against the Administration, the bans would stay in effect until the Supreme Court ruled on the merits later. This provided a resounding victory for the President in his attempts to protect the American people.

Only two justices, Sotomayer and Ginsberg dissented. The 7-2 margin poked a stick in the eye of activist judges, the ACLU and media. It demonstrated how far out of step they'd been ... apparently as a result of widespread TDS. This allowed Deplorables to say I-told-you-so once again but ... no ... we didn't tire of winning yet.

12/5/17: We were treated to more fake news ... ho hum. Bloomberg cited unnamed sources in reporting that Special Counsel Robert Mueller had subpoenaed Deutsche Bank for financial records of President Donald Trump. The media, Democrats and Left went crazy and began celebrating again. It only took a few hours for the Mueller team to confirm that they had not subpoenaed Deutsche Bank for the President's financial records. The TDS-deranged Left had grown desperate. There was no Russian collusion so instead of giving up and moving on, they switched gears and pursued obstruction of justice. All the while, obvious crimes by Hillary Clinton and other members of the Obama Administration were left unchecked.

The fix was in. After learning that a Hillary sycophant, FBI Agent Peter Strzok, had a lead role in the softball interview of Secretary Clinton during the email investigation and later harsh grilling of General Flynn, we found out that Special Counsel Mueller's Deputy, Andrew Weissmann, was also completely biased and on a personal crusade to help destroy President Trump.

Judicial Watch disclosed an email from Weissmann to then Acting AG Sally Yates in January 2017 after she exhibited brazen dereliction of duty under the Constitution and refused to uphold President Trump's travel ban. Weissmann's email breathlessly declared him to be so proud and awed by her act of TDS-driven defiance. He thanked her effusively and offered his deepest respects. This guy was second in command to Mueller in investigating President Trump! Deplorables recalled how Mueller picked a whole investigative team full of Hillary Clinton donors, staunch supporters and folks with ties to the Clinton Foundation. This thing stunk to high heaven and brought more calls to drain the swamp.

President Trump made the heads of lefty loons and enviromaniacs explode when he relaxed restrictions on millions of acres of public lands that had been ruled off limits by the Obama Administration. Demonstrating gross, perhaps willful ignorance and liberal mental illness, his detractors scolded the President for robbing the people and putting federal lands in jeopardy. These were some of the same people who thought tax cuts were pilfering from the federal Government as if the money belonged to the Feds who only in their beneficence gave some of <u>their</u> money to the unworthy, ungrateful citizenry. President Trump correctly pointed out that the Obama-era restrictions banned used of federal lands by the public. Ending these restrictions actually opened up use of these lands to the public. The President in effect said, *go ahead America ... enjoy <u>your</u> land again*!

12/6/17: President Trump made history and coincidentally shocked the public again by … gulp … keeping a well-known campaign promise. He officially recognized Jerusalem as the capital of Israel and vowed to move the U. S. Embassy there from Tel Aviv. On cue, Democrats, the media and numerous world leaders denounced the move as dangerous and a blow to the ongoing efforts to establish peace in the Middle East. President Trump correctly stated that fulfilling his campaign promise amounted to nothing more than the recognition of reality, both historical and current. He reaffirmed his commitment to seeking a lasting peace between the Israelis and Palestinians on the basis of a two-state solution.

The rabid criticism of the President's move proved once again that he could do no good … even if he cured cancer the TDS-infected Trump-haters would complain that he hadn't conquered asthma or acne. The irony and hypocrisy from the Left proved comically over-wrought. In 1995 the Congress had passed an overwhelmingly bi-partisan law called the Jerusalem Embassy Act that codified exactly what President Trump vowed to do. Various Presidents had promised to follow through but, unlike Donald Trump, had reneged on their word once elected. Instead, they had collectively signed a plethora of waivers to skirt the law.

People like Senator Dianne Feinstein who rushed to criticize the President and sounded alarm bells, apparently had short-term memory issues. Just six months prior the Senate had voted 90-0 in favor of S. Res. 176 that, among other things, reaffirmed the 1995 Jerusalem Embassy Act as U. S. law. Chicken Littles everywhere screeched that this would destroy the peace process. Deplorables said *what peace process?* For the past twenty-two years, Presidents had buried their heads in waivers while the so called peace process yielded bupkis. The Palestinians called for three days of rage thus showing that they had no interest in real peace. President Trump showed true wisdom by refusing to stay the course with a delusional policy that had only produced failure in attempting to secure a chance for true, lasting peace.

For those too deaf, dumb and blind to see, Rep. Al Green (D-Tex.) exposed the undeniable truth of the sole objective of loony, TDS-ravaged liberal Democrats. He introduced Articles of Impeachment against the President on the House floor citing as his rationale that President Trump was a bigot who incited hate and had demeaned the presidency. Never mind that the President had lowered black unemployment to record levels after the debacle of President Obama's eight years in office. Never mind that President Trump had a long history of supporting black civil rights going way back to at least 1997 when he filed a lawsuit against the City of Palm Beach to end discrimination against blacks and Jews.

In Green's deranged mind, Trump was a racist. Thankfully, even most Democrats were not yet willing to go this far. The House vote failed three-hundred-sixty-four to fifty-eight with Democrats siding with Republicans overwhelmingly. Still, Deplorables wondered how fifty-eight Dems could vote to impeach the President on these ludicrous grounds.

12/7/17: Disgraced Senator Al "He Who Gropes Sleeping Women" Franken used the Senate floor as a forum to announce his resignation. It seemed odd because he didn't really resign but promised to do so in the coming weeks. Deplorables asked *why the wait Al*? He went on defense by calling some allegations false and stated he remembered others differently than his accusers. I actually had some compassion for the man since he didn't receive due process. His fellow Democrats threw him under the bus for purely political reasons.

While the fabricated claims of Russian collusion floundered in a slow death spiral, the Democrats switched gears towards obstruction of justice; another hopeless red herring. Thinking ahead, it appeared the Dems wanted to set the table for sexual abuse charges by implying they'd cleaned their house of Franken, Conyers and others so why not President Trump? Franken erased any doubt about this theory by taking the opportunity to conflate his situation with the infamous Billy Bush NBC tape released during the 2016 campaign. There was only one problem. As crude as then Democrat Donald Trump's comments had been some twenty years ago, he never confessed to sexual harassment. He bragged crassly that women allowed him to grab their private parts because of his celebrity.

This sad commentary of those times unfortunately reflected the truth about human nature. People of both sexes would throw morality out the window if the temptation was right. That certainly included wealth and celebrity. Groping Al also conflated his transgressions with Roy Moore's alleged misdeeds in spite of a lack of hard evidence against him and Moore's total denial of the accusations. Franken tarred the entire GOP for embracing Moore despite widespread Republican calls for him to drop out of the race.

CNN couldn't stay on topic … sports … when they interviewed U. S. Skiing champion Lindsey Vonn about the upcoming Winter Olympics. They dove right into left-wing politics and asked her about representing President Trump in South Korea. Vonn obliged by stating she would be representing the United States but not our President, Donald Trump. She also said she would not visit the White House if invited by President Trump.

Did everything with the liberal media have to be about Trump-hate? The simple answer was yes. Just like with the NFL, they were now ruining the Olympics too. Deplorables wanted to caution Lindsey and CNN: *don't hold your breath waiting for an*

invitation to the White House from President Trump.
Somehow, despite my patriotism, I felt I couldn't root
for Lindsey in the Olympics.

12/8/17: Perhaps you had questioned my Deplorable
contention that modern-day liberalism was a mental
illness. If so, this day offered more proof for you.
Several activists, some associated with the NAACP,
called for a boycott of the upcoming opening of the
new Mississippi Civil Rights Museum because
President Trump announced his intention to honor the
event with his presence. Deplorables did a collective
double-take. The President of the United States
wanted to show his support and respect for African
Americans by taking time out of his busy schedule to
travel to Mississippi for the opening of a civil rights
museum and some liberal African Americans called
this move by the President an insult. I rested my case.

12/9/17: On the night before in Pensacola, Florida,
President Trump had given a stem winder to an
overflowing crowd who cheered raucously. Dave
Weigel of the Washington Post released a tweet that
called out President Trump for exaggerating the size
of the audience. He included a picture of the arena that

showed it about two-thirds empty. What he failed to reveal was that he took the photo two hours before the President spoke. Of course, the building was mostly empty at the time. President Trump called out Weigel publicly and demanded an apology. Weigel responded with sort of an apology calling his intentional fake news item a mistake and said the President was correct in calling him out.

Why couldn't the mainstream media just report the facts? Why did they have to go so far out of their way to spread lies in an attempt to discredit the President? It seemed like every other day someone in the media had to apologize or, like Brian Ross, be reprimanded for lying. Couldn't they grasp that they were only destroying their own credibility? Couldn't they see that they were reinforcing the fact that Donald Trump was only telling the truth when he called them fake news?

12/11/17: For eight excruciatingly long years of economic malaise, President Obama blamed everything on his predecessor, George Bush. Almost one year after leaving office, Barack Obama went public in taking credit for America's stunning economic turnaround under President Trump. So we were all supposed to believe that after nine years Obamanomics finally kicked in to reduce unemployment to the lowest level in seventeen years and generated over twenty-five record highs in the stock market. We were also to believe that consumer and business confidence reached record highs because people finally woke up and realized things were so great under Barack Obama.

When Donald Trump single-handedly eliminated a mountain of business-killing, Obama-era regulations, it somehow had nothing to do with the turnaround. Finally, it was strictly coincidental that the market skyrocketed every time it looked like tax cuts might get approved; tax cuts that Obama and his Dem pals like Nancy Pelosi referred to as Armageddon.

When President Trump recognized the obvious ... that Jerusalem was the capital of Israel ... Palestinians erupted with a multi-day fit of violence and their leader, Mahmoud Abbas, refused to meet with Vice-President Mike Pence. Never mind that most presidents and presidential candidates in the past twenty years had supported recognizing Jerusalem as Israel's capital and that the U. S. Senate had voted unanimously to support the same action only six months prior. The media spread the terrorist talking point that Donald Trump caused all the violence and hatred. President Trump and Vice-President Pence calmly stayed the course and reaffirmed their commitment to pursuing the peace process.

Hallelujah … we enjoyed a break from the media's deranged drumbeat against everything Trump. Wait … this wasn't good news because it took another terrorist attack to change the media's narrative. New York City suffered an ISIS-inspired bomb attack in the subway system near one of the busiest hubs by the Port Authority. Thankfully, the bomb detonated prematurely and only injured the perpetrator. He survived and provided authorities with a great chance to gather intelligence.

The question remained. Would they seize this opportunity and treat him like an enemy combatant or blow it by letting him lawyer up like a bank robber? In the meantime, it didn't take long though for the media to get back to normal. They quickly sided with the terrorist and implied that President Trump brought on this attack by recognizing Jerusalem as Israel's capital. No one mentioned gun control.

I wasn't a prophet but had a functioning brain. Therefore I offered this **FUTURE ALERT**. The Dems new strategy would pivot from Russian collusion and obstruction of justice. Those two approaches were as ineffective and hopeless as the ludicrous articles of impeachment vote that had gone down in flames recently.

From here on out, I believed the Dems and their media lackeys would make a major push to undermine the will of the people and the 2016 election results to oust President Trump on the basis of sexual improprieties. They had already rebooted the discredited female shills who they rolled out during the campaign. Never mind that the voters didn't bite before. It seemed to me that they considered this a winning hand and appeared ready to bet the house on it (pun intended).

In my opinion, this was why the Dems threw Senator Al Franken and Representative John Conyers under the bus. It also served as another reason why they waited so long to smear Roy Moore in a Clarence Thomas-style fashion. It coincided with their decision to stage their very own bimbo eruption in the midst of the man-hating hysteria that came to a boil in Harvey Weinstein's Hollywood and spread like wildfire from there.

In keeping with this theory, one of President Trump's accusers worked for the Clintons. Another accused Donald Trump of "inspecting" her during one of his beauty pageants. Imagine that ... hosts, judges, spectators and a huge television audience gave the once over to a beauty contestant ... shocking! Another one of the bimbos accused Donald Trump of kissing her on the lips. Wow ... I hoped they wouldn't make that a crime. Our prisons couldn't hold even a fraction of the "villains" who had committed this transgression. Here was the most important question. How many of the people who had made accusations against the President had been paid off by the likes of George Soros or the Clintons?

12/12/17: Authorities in NYC quickly ascertained that the bumbling subway bomber who proudly and

174

defiantly admitted allegiance to ISIS, Akayed Ullah, had legally emigrated from Bangladesh seven years prior via chain migration. At the head of the chain, his relatives came into the U. S. by winning the immigration lottery. While they hadn't yet figured out if he had become radicalized before or after coming to the U. S., President Trump promptly and correctly renewed his call for an end to chain migration. Why did Dems and establishment Republicans continue to resist any common sense attempt to enact obvious solutions? Why did they want open borders and favor policies that irrefutably put American citizens at risk?

Roy Moore lost the special senatorial election in Alabama by about twenty-thousand votes. Moore didn't concede stating that he wanted to wait until they tallied the military absentee ballots. Liberal puppet Doug Jones did not win because of the high turnout of Democratic voters although that certainly helped him. He owed his pyrrhic victory to some twenty-thousand Republicans who foolishly wrote in throw-away candidates like Alabama football coach Nick Saban on their ballots.

I called it a pyrrhic victory because I felt Jones' political career would be over in two short years when Jeff Sessions' remaining term ended. It was also pyrrhic for the American people. Jones' victory would make it that much harder for President Trump to carry out his agenda in making America great again. This all resulted from dubious claims from accusers who never made their case in a court of law. They didn't need to though since the court of an uninformed public opinion ruined Roy Moore without due process. I predicted Moore's accusers would now slink back into the shadows having carried out their political assassination successfully by duping voters with a big assist from the corrupt media. Deplorables shouted *thank you Alabama*!

12/14/17: Kyna Hamill, a professor of theatrical history at Boston University, declared *Jingle Bells* to be racist. Who would have thought that dashing through the snow in a one-horse open sleigh while laughing all the way had deep, disturbing racist undertones? I decided I must have been a racist because I had sung this delightful carol at least a thousand times and had even taught it to my grandkids. This would have been hilarious if not so serious.

Deplorables pondered the unfathomable. This nut case was teaching our young adults! If you were a parent shelling out your hard-earned dollars to send your kid to Boston University or just about any college in this land, this was what they were learning. If your kid was strapped with enormous college loan debt, did you think they would be able to dig themselves out by getting a high paying job spewing this kind of nonsense? At the risk of being repetitive I surmised again that … liberalism was a mental illness.

12/15/17: On the brink of nuclear war with North Korea, within days of possibly passing historic tax relief/reform legislation, with all of the serious news on the table, what did the lamestream media concentrate on? CNN thought it should make President Trump's consumption of a twelve-pack of Diet Coke a day their headline.

Others continued to waste time on what they deemed or hoped to be palace intrigue. Paul Ryan might be retiring as House Speaker in 2019, oh my!

Rex Tillerson was … again … rumored to be leaving his post as Secretary of State in 2018, oh no! Worst of all, Omorosa resigned her post as … uh; just what was her role in the White House? The latter generated the most chatter because, as a black, female, Democrat supporter of President Trump, the Left truly loathed her.

It appeared Chief of Staff John Kelly forced her to resign but the libs had no pity for Omorosa. They gleefully cheered her dismissal and scornfully implied she deserved her fate for betraying the "community." She had committed the unpardonable sin of not blindly supporting the Democrats even though they'd taken black voters for granted for the past sixty years while doing nothing to improve their lot in life. But wait; there was still hope for Omorosa. She hinted at a new book that most likely would be a turncoat hit piece on President Trump. If she did that, it would not only make her rich but the Left would do an about face and fawn over her.

12/17/17: Rep. Jackie Speier (D, CA) went on the Sunday shows to spread an unsubstantiated rumor that President Trump planned to fire Special Counsel

Robert Mueller on December 22nd while Congress recessed. She had no basis for making this claim and it could have been easily vetted by asking the President or someone on his staff but the liberal Press ran wild with it. It dominated the Sunday news until a reporter finally asked President Trump and he answered without hesitation that he would not fire Mueller.

While the biased, Trump-hating media chased this rumor down the rabbit hole and continued to deceive the American public, the big stories of the year went unreported. The economy boomed and stood on the brink of really taking off with the coming of historic tax reform. With their stronghold in Iraq and Syria in tatters and utterly defeated on the battlefield, ISIS had to disperse into the shadows to try to preserve their ideological caliphate through social media. Under President Trump's strong guidance, the United States vastly improved its national security by standing up to North Korea, Russia and China and reasserting itself as the leader of the free world.

In regard to tax reform, the media carried the Dems' water by spreading ludicrous lies that the tax cuts would only benefit the rich. They gleefully reported that polls showed most Americans believed the lie. When confronted with simple, irrefutable facts that lower and middle class Americans would benefit to the tune of $2,000 on average, they simply lied some more.

The mountain of evidence pointing to Watergate-style dirty politics and Russian collusion and obstruction of justice by Democrats continued to grow by leaps and bounds. A key member of Robert Mueller's investigative staff, Bruce Ohr, had not only met with Fusion GPS during the 2016 campaign but we also learned his wife had worked for Fusion GPS at the time. I couldn't make this up. Nellie Ohr's specialty at the firm that colluded with a British spy and the Russians to produce a phony, hit-piece dossier on candidate Donald Trump was ... drum roll ... Russian Politics. Yes, fact was stranger than fiction!

There was more. After seeing the texts exchanged between Trump-hating FBI investigator Peter Strzok and his mistress, we discovered they planned to consult with Andy (presumably Deputy FBI Director Andrew McCabe) to develop an "insurance policy" in case the unthinkable happened and Donald Trump won the election. That insurance policy no doubt included the fake Fusion GPS dossier and Russian collusion hoax. When asked if the FBI paid for the dossier, Deputy AG Rod Rosenstein said he knew the answer but wouldn't reveal it to the Judiciary Committee despite them having primary oversight over the Justice Department.

Deplorables recalled that McCabe's wife, Jill, had run for the Virginia State Senate and received $700 thousand in campaign support from uber-close Clinton ally, Governor Terry McCauliffe. We weren't fooled into thinking that Robert Mueller was above all of this. He had an axe to grind since President Trump interviewed him for the job of FBI Director and passed him over. The blood on his hands became evident when it was revealed recently that Mueller's team had surreptitiously obtained tens of thousands of Trump-associate emails by going around the Trump transition team to the GSA. Mueller's team whispered *nothing to see here folks*! The media helped with the diversion … *wait look over here at these shiny objects … Melania's Christmas decorations are ugly, the President drinks too much Diet Coke, the President plans to fire Mueller!*

12/18/17: On the lighter side, we learned that, thanks to Harry Reid, the government had used over $20 million in 2017 to chase down aliens. No, not the illegal aliens pouring across our southern border but little green men from Mars. Deplorables just had to shake our heads and laugh. These Dems had recently tried to portray themselves as fiscal hawks to trash the GOP's tax cutting plans. *Oh my, it's going to send the deficit through the roof!* Where were they when President Obama had doubled the $10 trillion in debt accumulated by all the other presidents combined in just eight years? Oh, they were following pie-eyed piper Harry Reid on a scavenger hunt for E. T.

12/19/17: Easthampton High School in Easthampton, Massachusetts banned the term "freshmen" in favor of "first year students" because they deemed the former as sexist. This followed the lead of Elon University in North Carolina three years prior when they banned "freshman" as a sexist term that promoted rape. I stopped laughing deplorably just long enough to state again that liberalism was a mental illness.

U. S. United Nations Ambassador Nikki Haley told the UN we'd be "taking names" as various countries prepared to vote on a resolution condemning America's decision to move its embassy from Tel Aviv to the capital of Jerusalem. President Trump had our feisty ambassador's back. He mentioned the billions of dollars we'd provided to the UN and dared them to vote against us and proclaimed it would be a good thing because we'd save lots of money. Deplorables everywhere released a collective sigh of blissful satisfaction at this refreshing, America-first attitude. After President Obama's eight-year-long apology tour, it felt good to hear our leaders tell the money grubbing malcontents at the UN to stick it where the sun didn't shine.

Why did the tax cut and jobs bill have to go back to the House of Representatives for a second vote? The answer was simply this: TDS-induced liberal insanity drove Democrats to put their Party's far-left ideology ahead of the good of the people they claimed to represent. After the House passed the bill and sent it to the upper chamber, they used arcane Senate rules to point out a couple of technicalities.

The "Byrd Rules" they employed originated under the late, longtime Democrat Senator Robert Byrd who had watched his Democrat colleagues use the race card over and over again while remaining mum on his past as an actual member of the KKK. They parsed words and forced the GOP-controlled Senate to revise the name of the bill. Then they objected to an add-on that allowed people to use tax-free 529 savings to pay for home schooling expenses. Yep, these champions of education denied home schoolers in order to pitch a last fit against middle-class tax cuts and economic growth.

12/20/17: Congressional investigators grilled Deputy FBI Director Andrew McCabe behind closed doors for seven and a half hours. Deplorables wondered why Democrats like McCabe received the privilege of appearing behind closed doors and pondered why no leaks occurred like they had whenever conservatives testified. This guy remained at the center of something so rotten the smell could not be dispelled by the media's most powerful air freshener.

Apparently, McCabe mostly stonewalled through the entire ordeal. Either he had something to hide or needed to be fired for incompetence. Deplorables concluded that the second in command at the FBI should not be clueless about his underling's schemes to devise an "insurance plan" in the event Donald Trump won the 2016 election, especially when Peter Strzok and company claimed to have hatched said plan under McCabe's supervision. This time, investigators didn't meekly accept the attempt to cover up the truth by remaining mum. They noted that his testimony contradicted that of other witnesses and ordered him to appear for a second round of questioning.

Deplorables marked this down as a red letter day. President Trump and conservatives set the foundation for a Deplorable victory in the 2018 mid-term elections. Congress passed the long-awaited tax cut and jobs bill they'd promised during 2016. Democrats voted unanimously in opposition to giving some of our money back to us.

Aided by their loyal lackeys in the media, Democrats had lied about the bill for six months citing their tired, old mantra that it would be a tax cut for the rich. Then they touted polls showing disapproval by the majority of Americans. Of course people who got their information from the

fake news media felt leery about a tax plan labeled as Armageddon by Nancy Pelosi and her ilk. The head of the resistance, obstructionist Senate Minority Leader Chuck Schumer, warned ominously that Republicans would rue the day they passed this bill.

Thankfully, President Trump and Republican congressional leaders didn't cave this time. They boldly placed their bet on the American people. They courageously said the truth would win out when people started seeing fewer taxes taken out of their paychecks in February or March 2018.

One Democrat spokesman summed things up well when he claimed some Democrats would have been on board if they had given the money back to "the people" instead of lowering corporate rates. When challenged that our corporate rates were not competitive with the rest of the industrialized world, he said they would have accepted a less aggressive lowering of corporate taxes if there had been provisions forcing corporations to do this or that with the savings. Voila ... he put it in a nutshell for us! Democrats believed in big government and not free enterprise. In exchange for providing a more competitive tax rate to our businesses, Dems wanted corporations to cede control over important business decisions to clueless bureaucrats in Washington, D. C.

Many Deplorables recalled how the media had made hay out of a supposed lack of support for the tax cuts among large corporations and laughed at how swiftly the truth came out. Within hours of the momentous bill's passage, a host of large corporations announced they would be sharing their gains with employees and reinvesting in growth that would mean jobs, jobs, jobs for Americans. For example, AT&T announced they would give $1,000 bonuses to all of their two-hundred-thousand employees. Now that's what I called trickle-down economics!

The same suspicions had prevailed, thanks to the media, when Ronald Reagan lowered taxes in the 1980s until the resulting economic boom yielded a landslide victory for him in the next election. The fact that every Democrat fought tooth and nail to stop tax cuts that would benefit all

Americans and promote incredible economic growth showed how far left they'd drifted. Whatever happened to the Party that produced John F. Kennedy and his massive tax cuts in the 1960s?

The tax bill included two other monumental Christmas gifts for the American people. The outsider, Donald Trump, broke with bad precedent again and ended some thirty years of liberal insanity by opening up a portion of the Arctic National Wildlife Refuge (ANWR) to drilling. For years, enviromaniacs had claimed that drilling for oil in ANWR would destroy the caribou and environmentally ruin a national treasure.

Although complete bunk, the public had bought into this nonsense thanks to the media's biased, irrational coverage. There were never any tourists visiting the oil rich part of ANWR and the caribou couldn't give a rip about drilling. The Alaskan people knew the truth and even RINO Lisa Murkowski applauded President Trump for finally unleashing the economic benefits hidden underneath the tundra.

In another brilliant move, the bill also put one of the final nails in the wretched Obamacare coffin by eliminating the individual mandate. This was really, really big folks. After much ballyhoo in the press about President Trump failing to fulfill his promise to repeal and replace Obamacare, they finally got it done. A lot of credit had to go to Mitch McConnell and the Republicans in the Senate who inserted this provision, much to delight of their House counterparts.

Armageddon Annie ... I mean Nancy Pelosi ... and other Dems labeled this as heartless. Of course, the media followed their pied pipers slavishly in condemning the move. Deplorables thought there was no better example of liberal insanity. They claimed to be for the little guy and young people. However, the individual mandate was a Democrat tax, as affirmed by the Supreme Court, designed to punish millions of people who didn't want or couldn't afford Obamacare. Poor people and young people who didn't need expensive, lousy Obamacare coverage had to pay thousands of dollars in penalties for the privilege of not having health insurance coverage. And the rest of us had to fill out more paperwork at tax time to prove we had insurance.

How about that for the party of choice? They'd give you the choice to murder your baby in the womb but wouldn't allow you to choose your own doctor and the level of coverage you preferred. People would not accept such nonsense if a morsel of truth was available. This just showed again that President Trump was right on target when he said some in the media were the enemy of the American people.

During his two terms, President Obama had done so many things to favor Muslim interests to the detriment of America's security and well-being that I didn't have enough space to list them all. It seemed like he got away with aiding and abetting our worst enemies time and again. However, it was worth noting that perhaps his pernicious deeds had finally caught up with him. Congress launched an investigation into bombshell revelations that President Obama had taken it easy on one of the worst terrorist groups on the planet, Hezbollah, in order to appease Iran.

Apparently, he had become so fixated with cementing his legacy, that he did anything and everything to secure the Iranian nuclear deal including sending pallet loads of cash that they used to finance their terrorist ambitions. The saddest thing about the whole sordid affair was that he had staked his legacy to what President Trump rightly called the worst deal in our nation's history. That was saying something when you considered that President Obama had traded five of the worst Islamic terrorist leaders at Guantanamo for the deserter, Bowe Bergdahl. How many more Americans died after these five scumbags returned to the battlefield? Only God knew.

12/21/17: Senator Bob Corker became a darling of the left-wing media when he broke with his GOP cohorts and participated in a very nasty, public feud with President Trump. Many thought he would vote against the tax cuts. However, after he became a yes, the same folks at CNN, et al that had fawned over him when he criticized the President did a hit piece on him.

They claimed that he switched positions for personal gain when the Senate added a provision that could benefit owners of income-generating real estate like Senator Corker. Although facts quickly showed that Corker had no knowledge of this provision when he decided to vote yes, the story made its way throughout the mainstream media. Senator Corker came out the next day and said he now understood how President Trump felt about the media and fake news.

The Democrats never quit. They'd become pathological liars. Days before, President Trump had attempted to put their loony tunes to rest when he stated emphatically he wouldn't fire Special Counsel Robert Mueller. I guessed Senator Mark Warner (Dem., VA) felt the need to deflect as the congressional investigators turned up the heat. After grilling Deputy FBI Director Andrew McCabe the first time, they put high-ranking DOJ Official Bruce Ohr on the hot seat. He was the guy who met with Fusion GPS, the creator of the nasty, fake dossier on Donald Trump. He was the same guy whose wife, Nellie, had worked for Fusion GPS as an expert in Russian politics.

As the noose slowly tightened, Warner stepped up to publicly decry any plan by President Trump to fire

Robert Mueller. Had he been sleeping when the President vowed not to do so? Did he think that vow should limit President Trump from pointing out the obvious that the deck had been stacked against him? Smart, informed people realized that, in spite of histrionics designed by people like Senator Mark Warner to distract the American people, the last thing President Trump wanted was to fire Robert Mueller. Mueller was in a position where he would either have to play it straight or ruin his own reputation completely. The President kept giving him more rope to hang himself.

There was no rest for the weary when it came to political games. Within hours of the GOP passing the first meaningful tax cut and jobs growth legislation in thirty years, the Democrats and their media allies poured cold water on the celebratory mood by force-feeding us news about a looming government shutdown. These Scrooges didn't care about Christmas. Calls for further resistance resounded.

After months of claiming President Trump hadn't delivered any major legislative victories, the Dems did their best to pooh-pooh this one of historic proportions. Deplorables like me didn't let this recurring nonsense ruin Christmas. We didn't give a hoot about shutting down our bloated government. We'd miss it about as much as being denied a slice of Aunt Bessie's stale fruitcake.

12/25/17: Partisan politics were laid aside for a few days while we celebrated the birth of our Lord and Savior, Jesus Christ … NOT! I was sorry to say that the hyper-partisan rankling didn't even pause on Christmas Day. I guessed that it was because the libs, by and large, didn't recognize Christmas any more than they respected God.

Deplorables marveled at this Christmas Day beauty. Authorities had to dispatch a bomb squad to investigate the situation after liberal loon neighbors of Treasury Secretary Steve Mnuchin sent a suspicious package to his Bel-Air home. Their "gift" of a box of horse manure also included a Christmas card laced with toxic comments about Mnuchin, President Trump and the recently passed tax cut bill.

California Governor Jerry "Moonbeam" Brown thumbed his nose at President Trump's immigration policy with this holiday offering. He pardoned two Cambodian men about to be deported for committing felonies in the U. S. One involved a weapons charge related to gang activity. I cringed at how this must have felt at Christmastime for the parents of Kate Steinle and others who had lost loved ones due to the insane policies of Gov. Brown and others who protected illegal immigrant criminals at the expense of American citizens.

Proving that TDS-induced, liberal mental illness wasn't limited to Democrats, RINO Arizona Senator and Never-Trumper Jeff Flake (appropriate last name) hinted at a possible presidential run in 2020. Deplorables tried to contain our spontaneous laughter.

United Airlines said bah humbug to teacher Jean-Marie Simon and bumped her from her first class seat in favor of Rep. Sheila Jackson Lee (D, TX). Congresswoman Lee was probably best known among Deplorables for competing hard with Congresswomen Maxine Waters (D, CA) and Frederica Wilson (D, FL with the rodeo clown cowboy hats) for the title of most deranged Trump-hater. When Rep. Lee's elitist behavior made the news, she responded reflexively by calling her detractors racially motivated.

One time professional comedienne Rosie O'Donnell did her best to kill the Christmas mood. The noted theologian ... nyuk, nyuk ... issued a Christmas Eve tweet proclaiming that Speaker Paul Ryan was headed straight to hell for cutting taxes. Even noted evangelist Franklin Graham felt compelled to take to social media to correct Rosie by reminding her she didn't hold the keys to hell.

The media didn't take off for the holidays either. They created a fake news firestorm by excoriating First Lady Melania Trump for cutting down the iconic magnolia tree on the White House lawn. They failed to mention that the National Park Service recommended that the dying tree be cut back for safety reasons. By following the Park Service's advice, the First Lady actually showed true compassion and impartiality since the Press often gathered beneath this tree while awaiting conferences with the President. Deplorables tried to imagine how they would have reported the First Lady's evil culpability if she'd left the tree standing and it fell on the Press Corp.

12/27/17: I marveled every time I thought about how President Bush never criticized President Obama after leaving office. Maybe I shouldn't have since apparently these men had more in common than I first imagined. In any case, I was truly amazed at the rapidity with which President Obama jumped back into the political fray to criticize President Trump and even audaciously tried to claim credit for the stunning economic turnaround that occurred as soon as Barack Obama vacated the White House.

Perhaps I shouldn't have been surprised since President Obama adhered to Alinsky's Rules for Radicals. Still, it was unsavory to say the least when a former president traveled abroad to undermine the sitting President of the United States. This time President Obama sat down with Prince Harry for an interview in which he criticized President Trump's policies. Such behavior seemed border-line treasonous to Deplorables.

12/28/17: Big-government, spend-happy Democrats had never seen a tax hike they didn't like. With the help of the media, they had always been able to sell their tax-and-spend philosophy by doling out freebies to the masses they'd kept in poverty-riddled dependence in spite of the glaring evidence of their policy failures in every Democrat-controlled major city. Donald Trump famously challenged this paradigm on the 2016 campaign trail by asking for urban voters to consider him by saying "What have you got to lose?"

Democrats thought they could win in 2018 by demonizing President Trump's and the GOP's tax overhaul as tax cuts for the rich. However, even with the media's help they could only hide the facts for so long. Data came out revealing a blue state exodus in 2017. Nearly four-hundred-fifty-thousand people left Democrat-controlled states due to crushing high taxes. New York lost one-hundred-ninety-thousand, California shed one-hundred-thirty-eight-thousand and over one-hundred-fourteen-thousand fled Illinois' exorbitant taxes. This happened before the tax cut bill passed.

Deplorables wondered what would occur now that fat cats in these blue states could only deduct up to $10,000 of their state and local taxes from their federal obligations. It seemed it would be extremely hard for the Dems to claim that high taxes weren't hurting their constituents. Moreover, it seemed regular folks would be more than a bit angry when they found out the Dems and their media lackeys had lied about the tax cuts being for the rich. When people saw more money in their paychecks through lower withholding, as *Ricky Ricardo* once famously said, the Dems would have some splaining to do.

1/2/18: We started off the New Year with some humor of the deranged kind that made us laugh until we cried. NBC News, fresh off the Matt Lauer debacle, decided to avoid future scandals by issuing some behavioral guidelines for employees to regulate their gender interaction. First they put the kibosh on romance in the workplace. That was worth a laugh wasn't it? Did they really think they could control powerful human emotions like love through policy edicts? Deplorable chortled *good luck with that*!

As if that wasn't enough, they took absurdity to another level by issuing a Standard Operating Procedure (SOP) for hugging. According to NBC News, hugging was only acceptable if done very briefly to avoid body contact. Huh ... wasn't that the whole point of hugging; body contact? As a topper, they actually offered this gem of advice for business lunches and dinners. Deplorables paused to listen with rapt attention. They said people should not take a vegan to a steak house. These were the people responsible for bringing us the mainstream news.

The State of Illinois offered up more comedy by declaring August 4th to be a state holiday: Obama Day. They chose the former President's birthday as the day to honor his legacy as a State Senator, U. S. Senator and U. S. President. The joke was on the citizens of Illinois because Obama Day would not entail a day off for government workers. Deplorables felt Illinois showed considerable bias since they failed to recognize another modern president who hailed from the Prairie State: Ronald Reagan.

Speaking of Barack Obama, it appeared he had taken the mantle from Hillary Clinton as the most noteworthy politician who refused to go away. Hillary seemed oddly absent as we turned the calendar to 2018. Perhaps she went into her cocoon when the congressional investigators and Justice Department turned up the heat by exploring the need to revisit the shady investigations that gave her a pass in 2016 and 2017.

President Obama seemed more than willing to fill the void. Beyond criticizing the Trump Administration abroad, he began to offer regular analyses of current policy decisions as if his opinion still mattered. He and his lying former cabinet member, Susan Rice, instructed President Trump that he should remain silent on matters such as the organic protests occurring in Iran.

This should have reminded the good people of Illinois just what kind of legacy President Obama had left us. In 2009 when Iranians took to the streets to protest their rigged elections, President Obama hadn't offered a peep of support for the masses. He had employed his normal practice of strategic patience which properly translated meant doing nothing. This so called champion of human rights had held his tongue when he had a chance to speak up for the downtrodden people of Iran so as to not upset the Mullahs with whom he desperately wanted to cut a nuclear deal so as to cement his wonderful legacy.

By the way, Vanity Fair forced Hillary out of hiding by releasing a tongue-in-cheek video that recommended she leave politics for knitting or some similar hobby. It must have shocked the failed presidential candidate to receive a smidgen of criticism, especially from a normally liberal stalwart like Vanity Fair. She responded by having her supporters criticize VF for sexism by noting that they didn't treat Mitt Romney the same way when rumors surfaced he might run to replace Orrin Hatch in the Senate.

The liberals in California must have noticed things weren't going so well. Their knuckleheaded policies such as becoming a sanctuary for illegal alien felons and onerous, business-destroying regulations caused tens of thousands to flee the state in 2017. How did they figure to turn the tide and get things back on track? No they didn't jump on the Trump Train. Instead, they thought it would help by legalizing recreational use of marijuana. Governor Moonbeam and his band of merry liberals in Sacramento showed themselves to literally and figuratively be real dopes.

If Hillary at least demonstrated the good sense of staying in the shadows as the pressure mounted, former FBI Director James Comey showed himself to be truly delusional or downright devious. As we rang in the New Year, he took it upon himself to tweet that he hoped 2018 would bring more ethical leadership to our country. Talk about the pot calling the kettle black! This guy hearkened back to Germany in the 1930s. Besides turning the FBI leadership into a politicized secret police force, he apparently modeled his communication skills after Joseph Goebbels. The NAZI propaganda minster was notorious for his tactic of accusing his opponents of the very transgressions he and his collaborators had committed. Comey's tweet caused Deplorables everywhere to ask … *hello, where were you AG Jeff Sessions, anybody home?*

President Trump thrilled Deplorables by speaking the truth to evil powers. He fired a New Year's Twitter storm at China, Pakistan, Iran and North

Korea. First the President said no more to the Chinese practice of promising one thing and doing another. Obama, both Bushes and Clinton had turned a blind eye to the obvious while kicking a can full of sewage down the road. When our satellites caught China transferring oil from their tankers into North Korean ships, President Trump called out China and President Xi.

Next he did something long overdue by threatening to withhold billions from Pakistan while correctly noting how they took our money but harbored terrorists fleeing from Afghanistan. And when the Iranian people rose up against the evil, theocratic regime in Tehran, he didn't leave them twisting in the wind like President Obama had done in 2009. He backed them up and criticized the regime for using the money gifted to them from President Obama to sponsor terrorists in Iraq, Syria, Yemen and elsewhere instead of helping their own people.

Finally, when Rocket Man issued a New Year's tweet that he had a button on his desk that could deliver a nuclear weapon to anywhere in the U. S., the President didn't cower in strategic silence. He fired off a tweet of his own noting that he too had a nuclear button; only much bigger and more powerful than the North Korean dictator's. Of course, liberal politicians and their media lackeys decried the President's bellicose tone but Deplorables everywhere raised a joint hallelujah.

While the media continued to bash President Trump for using such harsh rhetoric against North Korean dictator Kim Jong-un's nuclear threats, the Commander-in-Chief appeared to have proved his critics wrong yet again. Rocket Man picked up the hotline to South Korea for the first time in years and offered to hold talks with his rivals to the south. He even hinted at striking some kind of deal that would allow North Korea to participate in the upcoming Winter Olympics in South Korea.

1/3/18: Another sophomoric media tizzy exploded when someone, probably Michael Wolff's publicist, leaked comments attributed to Steve Bannon from Wolff's soon-to-be-released book, *Fire and Fury: Inside the Trump Whitehouse*. The media took the bait hook, line and sinker and greatly boosted the fortunes of what, by many accounts, amounted to nothing more than a trashy tabloid tell-all. The fake news intelligentsia looked right past several other prominent White House sources that labelled quotes from *Fire and Fury* as absolutely false. Instead, they glommed onto a quote from Bannon, the disgruntled and discredited former strategist, where he used the explosive term "treasonous" to describe the meeting between Jared Kushner, Donald Trump Jr. and the shady Russian lawyer lady who we later found out seemed to be in cahoots with the Clinton Team.

Had they forgotten how just three months prior Bannon had gone on *60 Minutes* and bashed the Russian collusion story as nonsense? Prior to Wolff's highly suspect revelation, the media had branded Bannon as Hitler reincarnated or the spawn of Satan. By betraying and bashing President Trump, he suddenly became a media darling. True to form, the media set aside serious issues like the looming nuclear menace of North Korea, the January 19th budget deadline and immigration reform to go gaga over salacious tripe.

President Trump for his part didn't back down. He rightfully blasted the narcissistic Bannon by saying he had not only lost his job but his mind too. He then instructed his lawyers to file a cease-and-desist order against Bannon for violating the terms of his NDA. The media immediately launched into their Trump is mentally unfit mantra while Deplorables applauded the President for defending his family's honor so forcefully. President Trump put the icing on the cake by labeling Bannon as "Sloppy Steve."

U. N. Ambassador Nikki Haley announced the U. S. planned to withhold $255 million in security aid from the Palestinians. The Palestinian Authority had a hissy fit and the mainstream media chimed in claiming that President Trump would only drive refugees into the arms of the extremists. Thankfully, the President didn't back down.

Deplorables breathed a sigh of relief at this refreshing turn of events. Finally, a U. S. President had the courage and common sense to do the right thing. President Trump rightly noted that it made no sense to shower the Palestinians with more millions while they refused to participate in the peace process. Why finance their efforts to foment more violence?

It was no laughing matter when Minnesota Congressman and DNC Deputy Chairman Keith Ellison threw his support behind an Anti-Fa handbook promoting the use of violence against President Trump and his supporters. Ellison, the only Muslim in the House of Representatives, already had a reputation for supporting extremist causes including Louis Farrakhan and the Nation of Islam but this took his radical views to a new level.

Everyone had seen the kind of violence carried out by Anti-Fa, the anti-fascists who were actually fascists. But had the Democrat Party really shifted this far to the left that they elected a Deputy Chairman who openly supported an Anti-Fa group whose activities had rightly been labeled as domestic terrorist violence by the FBI? Sadly, it was true.

ESPN continued to pose as a sports network despite being, in reality, a left arm of the Democrat Party. One of their unhinged talking knuckleheads, Max Kellerman, went ballistic on the Houston Astros for committing the unpardonable sin of accepting an invitation to visit the White House in recognition of their World Series championship … gasp! Mad Max said the Astros were on the wrong side of history. Deplorables recognized this aberrant behavior as TDS-induced hyperbole.

1/4/18: Whether humor or insanity, the comedy continued; this time from actress Meryl Streep. She lit into Melania Trump and Ivanka Trump for their silence on sexual abuse. Apparently, she felt the two women were complicit because they didn't support the fake news about Donald Trump having sexually abused various women; some of whom were bribed by the likes of Lisa Bloom to level their bogus charges.

Deplorables needed sharp knives to cut through the hypocrisy. Just a month prior, Meryl Streep had been roundly criticized for covering up the rampant sexual misconduct of Harvey Weinstein to further her own career. In 2012 while accepting her Best Actress Award at the Golden Globes, she referred to the movie producer as god. That was an insult to false gods everywhere and the true God just laughed in derision.

Deplorables marked this down as another monumental day for the cause of freedom and

thanked feisty California Congressman Devin Nunes for his dogged determination. It appeared that some semblance of justice had gained a little traction after years of Deep State stonewalling and cover-ups. News reports, at least on FNC, said the FBI had decided to take a fresh look at the Clinton email scandal and alleged pay-for-play schemes run through the Clinton Foundation. This came on the heels of the release of Huma Abedin's emails showing she had transmitted confidential information to her husband Anthony Wiener's unsecured laptop. Deplorables recalled that Abedin served as one of Hillary Clinton's top aides and former Rep. Wiener now resided in prison for sexual misconduct.

Also, thanks to the herculean efforts of Judicial Watch, a court ruling finally came down to allow the shedding of light on Fusion GPS's bank records. Would we finally find out if the FBI used the fake dossier to gain warrants to spy on the Trump campaign? Would Hillary and her gang be subjected to the same scales of justice as the rest of us? Deplorables cautioned *not so fast folks*. Unfriendly leaks continued to pour from the

Justice Department under AG Jeff Sessions' lax leadership.

The latest fake news out of the failing New York Times tried to derail the truth train by citing four unnamed FBI sources who claimed that it wasn't the fake dossier funded by the Clinton campaign that initiated the Russian collusion investigation. No, it all started when a drunken wannabe Trump advisor George Papodopoulos bragged about the Trump campaign having dirt on Hillary Clinton to an Australian diplomat in a London wine bar. This supposedly caused the Australian government to advise the Obama Administration who then sprang into action. Not many people bought into this hogwash but it didn't stop the Left from trying to get the hounds off the right trail. Fusion GPS continued their resistance by trying to appeal to a higher court to continue their cover-up.

For his part, AG Jeff Sessions went off on another tangent by declaring the Justice Department intended to uphold federal law despite several states bucking the system to legalize marijuana. Under normal circumstances, this would have been a welcome development after years of President Obama legislating from the Oval Office. Instead of having the President tell the Feds to ignore the rules pertaining to illegal substances, the AG now made headlines with the novel idea of actually enforcing the laws on the books; laws properly enacted by Congress. However, this seemed like a very odd time to make this move.

Could Sessions actually be part of the move to divert attention with another shiny object? Thankfully, conservative bulldog Congressman Jim Jordan issued a call for AG Sessions to do his job or resign. All things considered, the events of this day truly seemed to amount to a game changer. Oh, by the way, had you heard about the fire at the Clinton's Chappaqua home? The fire hadn't occurred in the main house but rather on the second floor of the separate structure used to house the Secret Service. Hmmmm, the Clinton's wouldn't stage a fire to get rid of more evidence, would they?

1/5/18: Evoking memories of Jemele Hill's earlier vulgar diatribe against the President, ESPN's Katie Nolan referred to Donald Trump as a blanking "stupid person." Yes, I bleeped out the F-bomb she dropped on air. When was ESPN going to change their name to Entertainment, Sports and Political News? Did they really think people tuned in to watch TDS-impaired nitwits spew their hatred of the President and force their uninformed left-wing lunacy down our throats? We just wanted to see a game and escape from hyper-partisan politics for a while! Was that too much to ask from a sports network? No wonder ESPN's ratings continued to plummet.

ESPN's brass let Nolan off with a gentle reprimand. They didn't even suspend her! When did it become okay to drop F-bombs on TV, especially a sports network viewed by a lot of kids? On top of that, when did it become fashionable to disrespect the President of the United States using gutter language?

ESPN also demonstrated their desire to be just like the mainstream media by specializing in fake news. For example, they concocted a salacious story about how the New England Patriots were being ripped apart at the seams by jealousy and intrigue between Owner Robert Kraft, Head Coach Bill Belichick and Quarterback Tom Brady. Yeah, that was the ticket. When people turned the dial to ESPN to see football, baseball, basketball and hockey, ESPN dumped on the President, forced their political ideology on pathetic Deplorables and killed the golden goose with tabloid nonsense.

Chip and Joanna Gaines announced they were expecting their fifth child. They had recently fallen prey to speculation about marital problems as the motivation for their decision to end their popular HGTV show *Fixer Upper*. Rumor mongers in the voyeuristic media couldn't accept their explanation that they wanted to spend more time with their children.

Announcing the pregnancy quelled the irresponsible rumors, right? Wrong ... the haters just shifted the focus of their negative energy. While most normal people and fans of the show offered congratulations, some twisted people took to social media to scold the couple for contributing to the world's supposed overpopulation. Why, you might have asked, was this nonsense worthy of inclusion in this chronology? I think it perfectly captured the mindset of the liberal Left and their culture of death.

God said, be fruitful and multiple ... and added not to worry because He would provide for our needs. More than anything else, Progressives were in rebellion against God and His ways. They argued that we must limit population growth because of overcrowding and starvation. That worthless theory was debunked back in the early 1800s when Thomas Malthus predicted gloom and doom. It was made to look completely foolish when Paul Ehrlich tried to revive this Chicken Little hypothesis in 1968 with his book The Population Bomb. He assured us that the overcrowded world would face mass starvation in the 1970s and 1980s. Instead, today one of our greatest problems was obesity ... go figure.

Similarly, we were freezing our hind ends off in the U. S. this winter despite Al Gore's assurances that the polar ice caps would be gone years ago. We could laugh at Uncle Al's comic crusade against climate change but the culture of death was another matter. The people who wanted to shame the Gaines for having a fifth child would have preferred to see their baby put to death along with the other million-plus abortions each year in the name of choice and for the supposed good of mankind. They mourned the "death" of a tree or furry forest creatures but had no sympathy for human beings. Deplorables weren't fooled by their rationalizations. Far-left loons hated God and wanted nothing but death for the crown of His creation: mankind.

A Washington State Sheriff's Deputy was killed in the line of duty while responding to a home invasion. At the time of this writing, a massive manhunt was underway for the two burglars who shot and killed the officer as he pursed them. I included this entry just to remind everyone that the war on cops hadn't slowed down a bit. Deplorables didn't need to be reminded further by me citing the numerous, almost daily tragedies of this sort. Why didn't Dems call for gun control when cops were killed???

I didn't waste my time watching the Golden Globe Awards since they mainly served as a bad excuse for a political convention of Hollywood elitist liberals. However, I couldn't dodge them completely thanks to the mainstream media coverage. From what I gathered, it basically represented a Trump hate-fest … ho hum. Hyper-hypocrisy was in full bloom when the starlets wore their Me Too little black dresses to supposedly stand up for oppressed, sexually-harassed women. Of course, this left out conservative women, Muslim women and Bill Clinton's victims. It also sidestepped the ticklish issue of dealing with Meryl Streep's god, Harvey Weinstein. The most noteworthy manifestation of mass-TDS and slavish devotion to the Democrat Party came when the host anointed Oprah Winfrey as the next President of the U. S.

To top things off, the Hollywood hypocrites showered Tonya Harding with love and depicted her as some kind of victim while they feted her biopic, *I Tonya*. They apparently ran short of sympathy when it came to the real victim, Nancy Kerrigan, who was attacked by Tonya's thuggish husband in an attempt to knock her out of the 1994 Olympic competition in one of the worst examples of poor sportsmanship in history. Allison Janney won a Best Actress award for portraying Tonya's mother who got thrown under the bus in *Mommy Dearest* fashion to justify Harding's despicable behavior.

It had started with the Russian collusion hoax. While some still tried to beat this dead horse, most gave up based on the never-ending Mueller investigation that hadn't turned up a shred of evidence. Still, CBS tried their best at a last gasp effort on *60 Minutes* by attempting to ambush the head of Russia Today (RT), Margarita Simonyan. I had to laugh as the young Russian ran circles around robotic, doddering Leslie Stahl.

In truly a pot-calling-the-kettle-black interview, Stahl hurled one unsubstantiated claim after another that sounded more like a true confession than a gotcha moment. Lib Leslie accused RT of propaganda while failing to notice her and her colleagues' own image in the mirror. She denounced RT for supporting Donald Trump. Simonyan deftly pointed out that RT's transgression amounted not to supporting Donald Trump but rather their lack of support for Hillary Clinton. She applied the coup de grace by pointing out how CBS didn't seem to mind how French President Macron tried to influence our election by openly supporting Hillary.

I almost felt ashamed as I cheered for the Russian as she flayed the American hypocrite but I had to sadly admit that our Russian nemesis had the truth on her side on almost every point contended. Despite Simonyan's burial of Leslie Stahl, I hesitated to call Russian collusion a dead horse. Maybe a cat was a better metaphor because the Russian hoax seemed to have at least nine lives. Maybe that was because there wasn't a better alternative. Obstruction of justice claims failed miserably as a replacement and contrived sex scandals couldn't seem to gain traction.

The latest switcheroo from the Resistance appeared to have more momentum. Deplorables could hear the growing chant coming from all quarters of liberal la-la land. Trump was crazy … he was unfit for office … he was going to destroy the universe if they didn't stop him. A week earlier, the mainstream media, as if on cue, had regurgitated the story of how some nutcase psychiatry professor from Yale named Dr. Brandy X. Lee (sorry but this sounded like a porno star) had briefed twelve members of Congress (eleven Dems and one RINO) on President Trump's mental health. This "expert" said, "From a medical perspective, when we see someone unraveling like this, it's an emergency. We've never come so close in my career to this level of catastrophic violence that could be the end of humankind."

And insane liberals took this stuff seriously. The media clamored to see the results of the President's latest physical to see if it would confirm he'd gone bonkers. Then the media let Michael Wolff's book drown out every other form of meaningful news. Never mind that the author of this pack of lies had little credibility even in liberal circles. It questioned President Trump's fitness for office and thus supported their latest narrative and effort to overturn the will of the American people.

1/9/18: It didn't take President Trump long to blow the Left's mental instability theory out of the water. In classic Trump fashion, he turned conventional wisdom on its head and used the media to destroy the media-inspired false narrative regarding his mental condition. The President called a bi-partisan group of leaders from the House and Senate together to kick off negotiations regarding immigration reform and the looming government shutdown threatened by the Democrats. Instead of asking the

Press to leave after some opening remarks, he allowed full transparency for fifty-five minutes of negotiations. Everyone, including the media, hung on every word as both sides pitched their positions in a fascinating public discourse unlike anything we'd seen in modern American political history.

There was no sane way to deny the President's leadership, poise, graciousness and willingness to compromise. This was no unhinged, ill-equipped, stumbling buffoon. President Trump showed himself to be clearly in command and leaders from both sides could not help but afford him proper deference. Some on the Left still tried to spin this amazing display as somehow a negative reflection on the President but even the likes of CNN had to uncharacteristically offer a few positive remarks about his performance.

Some on the right, including me, worried that President Trump had been suckered into a fool's game like President Reagan who agreed to amnesty up front while the Dems got off scot free with hollow promises about border security coming later. However, I didn't fall into a panic like Ann Coulter and some others. When Senator Dianne Feinstein channeled Popeye's pal Wimpy ("I will gladly pay you Tuesday for a hamburger today.") with a request for a "clean DACA bill" the President appeared to consent. But he later cleared up any misunderstanding by stating he understood a clean DACA bill to mean DACA plus border security including the wall and an end to chain migration and the visa lottery system.

I felt reassured as I reflected on the unprecedented public meeting. President Trump painted another masterpiece as Dealmaker-in-Chief. He killed the vicious rumors, made Michael Wolff irrelevant and demonstrated true statesmanship while almost surely ensuring a victory for his conservative agenda. Sure, he had to give in on DACA but that was a foregone conclusion based on popular opinion among Democrats and Republicans. But instead of horse trading on DACA to simply keep the government from shutting down, he set the wheels in motion to possibly achieve major immigration reforms that all of his predecessors failed to enact ... since their hearts really weren't set on slowing down illegal immigration.

1/10/18: Speaking of Senator Feinstein, she showed her true colors a day later and earned the moniker of "Sneaky Dianne" from the President by taking it upon herself to release a transcript of the Judiciary Committee's interview of one of Fusion GPS's founders, Glenn R. Simpson. This served to kill the bi-partisan good will created the day before since she acted without consulting Chairman Chuck Grassley or any of her other Republican colleagues on the Committee. The transcript offered nothing of true evidentiary importance regarding the Russian collusion illusion but cast light on testimony from Mr. Simpson where he tried to burnish the reputation of Fusion GPS and their British spy, Christopher Steele, as unbiased, impeccable researchers.

At first, Senator Feinstein reacted to the storm of criticism she received by saying she felt her revelation had served the purpose of full transparency. That didn't fly since the transcript was heavily redacted and made people wonder what secrets had been blotted out. Then "Sneaky Dianne" came back a day later and sort of apologized for going around her colleagues by stating perhaps her mental capacity had been reduced by a severe cold.

As if "Sneaky Dianne's" runny nose excuse wasn't enough, we were treated to two other noteworthy examples of liberal lunacy on the same day. First, Math Professor Laurie Rubel of Brooklyn College said in an article in the Journal of Urban Mathematics Education that meritocracy in math class was a "tool of whiteness." Wow ... who knew that math was behind racism all along? Thus two-plus-two equaled four only if you were white. She went on to say that math had been used to erect "systematic barriers" against, I guessed, social justice. This didn't exactly thrill people who were paying their hard earned money or going into deep debt to get a college degree.

The topper came from Robert De Niro who, I must admit, had been one of my favorite actors of all time prior to him going off the deep end in 2016. Then he had contracted a severe case of TDS. The man who had soared in such classic films as the *Godfather*, *Deer Hunter* and *Goodfellas* went before the National Board of Review of Motion Pictures during their annual awards ceremony and self-destructed. Unable to contain his viral hatred, he launched into a profanity-laced tirade against President Trump that dropped the F-bomb and other expletives. I couldn't laugh since it disheartened me to see one of my silver screen heroes utterly obliterate a stellar reputation he'd richly earned over many decades. It showed the sad, depressing side of liberal mental illness when such an otherwise brilliant individual lost his mind completely over something as silly as an extreme political ideology.

1/11/18: Things took a hard turn from insane comedy to serious news a day later when Sara Carter of Circa News revealed what had seemed inevitable to clear-thinking individuals for weeks. She stated that reputable, highly placed sources within the FBI and Justice Department confirmed that they had used the fake dossier manufactured by Fusion GPS to, in part, justify and secure the warrants used to spy on the Trump campaign. This was no shiny object like the Russian hoax or false narrative created by Michael Wolff to question the President's mental fitness. Finally, solid evidence of Watergate-like election abuses and actual Russian collusion by the Clinton campaign had surfaced.

This left Deplorables with two burning questions. Why did this have to come from an investigative reporter at Circa News rather than the Special Counsel or plethora of congressional committees supposedly studying the Russia claims? Would indictments or a grand jury follow? I still had great doubts since desperate Robert Mueller now clamored, with the help of the Press, for an interview of President Trump.

Why in the world would the President consent? Since Mueller had produced no evidence of collusion between Russia and the Trump campaign, it appeared he hoped to catch the President in a perjury trap if he could trick him into misspeaking. President Trump rightly pointed out that Hillary Clinton had been treated with kid gloves: no recording, no transcript or notes, no oath and the softball interview had been buried during the 4th of July holiday by agents sympathetic to the Clinton campaign.

It became increasingly difficult for the Dems and mainstream media to ignore the immediacy of the incredible success of the Trump tax cuts. They had largely ignored or under-reported a flood of corporations that gave some of the tax savings back to their employees in the form of bonuses, benefits and higher wages. It didn't fit the narrative that corporations would take their tax windfall and give it all back to fat cat shareholders in the form of dividends or stock buy backs.

Things really blew up in their faces when one of their favorite mantras crumbled. Libs had constantly clamored for mandatory increases in minimum wages in spite of clear evidence that doing so would only result in lost jobs. Walmart often served as one of their pet targets of supposed corporate greed. They must have been shocked when Walmart, the nation's largest private employer, announced they would voluntarily increase their minimum wage to $11.00 per hour and offered $1,000 bonuses to their employees along with enhanced benefits such as greater maternity leave ... all as a result of the tax cuts.

To make matters worse for anti-capitalist liberals, Jack-in-the-Box came out the same day and announced they would be cutting jobs in favor of robots as a result of government-imposed minimum wage hikes. Liberals never learned. They ignored the definition of insanity: repeating the same behavior over and over while expecting different results.

For his part, President Trump kept touting the success of his economic policies even though the truth he spoke often fell on deaf ears. He took particular pride in noting how unemployment among blacks had dropped to its lowest level in recorded history (1972) in just eleven months under his leadership. Even though the media ignored this good news, apparently some people on the street still took note. They didn't fall for the nonsense that President Obama's feckless policies had finally kicked in after eight long years.

Some recalled Donald Trump's campaign challenge to minorities, "What have you got to lose?" One poll showed that eleven percent of African-American women no longer held a preference for the Democrat Party. Sometimes the truth did win out, despite all the propaganda the media served up.

1/12/18: Things changed fast in the 24/7 fake news cycle. The DACA deal based on "love", as President Trump deemed it, headed south in a hurry. To their credit, the bi-partisan team assembled by the President came up with a swift response to his call for a DACA deal. To their discredit, they ignored the four pillars everyone had supposedly agreed to … DACA, border security, ending chain migration and dropping the visa lottery … and plopped such a bad proposal on the President that he went ballistic.

He used some harsh language in denouncing their response and detractors led by Dick Durbin immediately leaked to the Press that President Trump labelled certain point-of-origin nations as expletive-holes. This took center stage as one news outlet after another sensationalized the situation before checking the facts. President Trump tweeted that he used tough language but not the expletive assigned by the leaker. Did it really matter?

The media overlooked the common sense employed by the President, however crude it might have been: why should the United States accept the dregs instead of using a merit-based immigration system? To make matters worse ... and more comical ... Nancy Pelosi chimed in and criticized President Trump's bi-partisan effort as "five white guys." Even Steny Hoyer had some unkind words for his Democrat colleague for playing the race and feminist cards. Perhaps he disliked being on the receiving end along with the usual Republican targets.

Pelosi went on to say that the bonuses being handed out by corporations to employees amounted to **"crumbs."** There you had it folks! Some people ... in this case, the whole Democrat Party ... never learned. Her first mistake was labeling the tax cut plan as Armageddon. When numerous corporations swiftly proved her wrong by volunteering to give $1,000 - $3,000 bonuses to employees along with other enhanced benefits, she turned up her nose and called them **crumbs**.

In one brief statement to the Press she exposed her elitism by calling us all Deplorables again. We were racists, misogynists and stupid on top of it because we let the big corporations dupe us with their **crumbs**. I guessed that to a person who somehow accumulated hundreds of millions of dollars while serving in Congress, $1,000 - $3,000 amounted to **crumbs**. We Deplorables had some news for Nancy: a thousand bucks made a big difference to forgotten middle-Americans who worked their butts off to make ends meet.

1/13/18: I hated wasting more ink on such nonsense but felt compelled to add another entry since the fake news media continued to froth at the mouth over President Trump's alleged blank-hole comment over the weekend. CNN and all the other loony-liberal news outlets tried their best to outdo each other with over-the-top charges of racism against the President. Somehow they missed the subtle but crucial point that the President had referred to countries and not people. They also ignored that Dick Durbin served as the only eyewitness to claim that Donald Trump used the blank-hole term and

Durbin had a long history of embellishing things to twist the truth.

In any case, Deplorables wanted to know why it was racist to ask the question of why America should take in immigrants from hell-hole countries (sanctimonious Lindsey Graham's term) or blank-show countries (President Obama's term for Libya) rather than using a merit-based system to welcome people. Deplorables also wanted to know when Dems suddenly became moralistic about the use of foul language. Since when was plain, common sense logic, regardless of the salty language involved, racist? It didn't matter to the Trump-hating Press though. They piled on with one racist claim after another and one NPR host, Maria Hinojosa (who?), went so far as to call ICE Agents the Gestapo for enforcing immigration laws. Deplorables scratched their heads because, to them, Haiti <u>was</u> a hell-hole.

If Deplorables had any doubts about the Dems' true motivation, the poster child for doddering liberal lunacy cleared things up when Nancy Pelosi took to the podium to call for a clean DACA bill. Liberals didn't give a damn about Haiti, Africa or so-called Dreamers for that matter. They cared about votes and politics, period. They took Tricky Dicky Durbin's breach of confidence and ran with the race card to try to reshape negotiations. The topper occurred when Chelsea Clinton came out to denounce President Trump as somehow insensitive toward Haitians. Deplorables recalled how the Clinton Foundation ripped off the Haitians to help make it more of a hell-hole and they purportedly used $3 million of donations to pay for Chelsea Clinton's wedding while disaster-ravaged Haitians suffered.

1/14/18: I dedicated this entry to the 24/7 news cycle. It used to be that we'd get a break from the constant barrage of fake, absurd, serious, shocking, distressing and ominous news on the weekends but no more. This weekend featured a little of everything. On the serious side, Hawaii understandably went into a state of panic when some knucklehead pushed the wrong button and sent out an automated alert of an incoming missile attack. Following the Democrat axiom of never letting a good crisis go to waste, Rep. Tulsi Gabbard took things from serious to absurd when she blamed the problem on President Trump even though Hawaii's bureaucracy admitted they'd erred. No, I wasn't kidding.

We couldn't go a day without some fake news when the wrangling continued over President Trump's purported blank-hole, racist comment. Senators David Perdue and Tom Cotton who also attended the infamous meeting claimed the President never used the blank-hole term and stated that Tricky Dicky Durbin had grossly misrepresented President Trump's remarks. For his part, the President said DACA was probably dead. The guy never stopped posturing and negotiating on behalf of the American people.

In the strictly laughable category, David Letterman, looking like Rip Van Winkle, interviewed President Obama who continued his private war against Fox News and Deplorables by stating that people who watched FNC were from "another planet." The mainstream media somehow missed the hypocrisy overflowing from a former President who had been severely critical of Donald Trump for attacking the media. Deplorables snickered at the sight of Obama and Letterman pretending to still be relevant.

President Trump must have wondered why he ever tried to reach for a bi-partisan solution on DACA after being stabbed in the back by Tricky Dicky Durbin. If he had any doubts about the futility of dealing with the mindless Democrat resistance movement, Representatives Maxine Waters and John Lewis announced their intention to boycott the President's first State of the Union Address. Deplorables marveled at the childish madness on full display in the U. S. Congress. Why were we paying the do-nothing Dems in Congress who had even opposed tax cuts for the middle class and poor in order to spite President Trump?

Not everything was lighthearted or loony. Deplorables ominously noted that YouTube, Google and Facebook all had implemented measures to censure harmful or offensive information that just happened to reflect conservative viewpoints. FNC host Pete Hegseth had a video pulled as inappropriate because he documented how military gains in Iraq and elsewhere in the Middle East under

President Bush had been lost during President Obama's term. Dennis Prager of conservative Prager University decided to sue YouTube for restricting numerous videos as offensive or inappropriate including even a series on the Ten Commandments. Deplorables felt a terrible chill down their spines at the mounting evidence of big brother controlling thoughts and information flow via the media, academia and now social media powerhouses like Google, Facebook and YouTube.

Last but not least, we had a smattering of good news of the kind largely unreported. The investigation into the corrupt Clinton Empire seemed to be building momentum as the first indictment was handed down in regard to the Uranium One scandal. The media also tried to stem the tide of more encouraging economic news when Fiat Chrysler announced it would bring some production back from Mexico to the United States along with two-thousand-five-hundred jobs. The media just couldn't stand to admit that, once again, the President had been right all along that deregulation and tax cuts would bring offshore jobs and money flowing back into America.

1/16/18: Sometimes, in the midst of all the insanity, it was helpful to simply let numbers speak for themselves without a bunch of rhetoric. Several things jumped out at me on this day. First, four more police officers were shot in York, SC while responding to a domestic violence call. Also, a media study for 2017 showed that President Trump received ninety percent negative coverage for the full year. Finally, an earlier report had the President's support among African-American women up from four to eleven percent. A new study revealed that black men had also upped their support of Donald Trump from eleven to twenty-three percent. This proved that people were smarter than Democrats thought. They listened to their wallets more than the fake news media.

Three-term White House Physician, Dr. Ronny Jackson took to the podium before Sarah Huckabee Sanders' press conference to share the results of President Trump's first annual physical examination. In effect, the President poked a stick into the eye of the media and all the Democrats who tried to create the illusion of an unhealthy, mentally unstable

Donald Trump by asking the doctor to publicly share his results in minute detail.

The only negative finding was, not surprisingly, that the President could stand to lose a few pounds and lower his cholesterol a bit more. However, President Trump had excellent cardio health which the doctor attributed to good genes and abstinence from any alcohol or tobacco use in his life. In short, the doctor pronounced the seventy-one-year-old President to be in amazingly good health.

Most importantly, President Trump scored a perfect thirty out of thirty on his cognitive test. The Press responded by asking questions about the President's ice cream intake and challenged Dr. Jackson's credibility. Deplorables wondered what kind of scores the mentally ill liberals in the Press Corps would have received from the same cognitive test.

1/17/18: Outgoing AZ Senator Jeff "Snow" Flake took to the Senate floor and gave a speech denouncing President Trump through a myriad of supposed transgressions while comparing him to

Joseph Stalin. This disgusting display proved three things. First, Flake was a coward who only challenged the President with his deranged, personal vendetta after he'd already thrown in the towel when he ascertained that the voters of Arizona would no longer put up with his antics. Second, he was a disingenuous, liberal Democrat posing in GOP sheep's clothing. Finally, he had no business being part of the Gang of Six seeking a "bi-partisan" deal on DACA, border security and immigration reform. For that matter, Deplorables wanted to know how the Gang of Six could be considered bi-partisan when there was only one marginal Republican in the group, Colorado Senator Cory Gardner. Flake and Lindsey Graham didn't even qualify as RINOs.

As the DACA debate raged on and yet another government shutdown crisis loomed, people understandably but foolishly longed for our great national wound to be healed. Such wishful thinking proved futile because there could be no compromise between good and evil. Two diabolical examples put this tragic state of affairs into sobering perspective.

The first one sent chills down everyone's spines ... except the most corrupt, vote-mongering Dems ... when courtroom video showed a stunningly matter-of-fact outburst from Luis Bracamontes during his trial for the October 2014 murders of two California Sheriff's Deputies. He laughed derisively and flashed a devilish grin and proclaimed "I wish I could have killed more of those mother_____." He added, "I will break out soon and I will kill more, kill whoever gets in front of me." Luis Bracamontes was an illegal alien who had been arrested and deported multiple times prior to his bloody rampage. This man was truly beyond redemption, humanly speaking. Only Jesus Christ could save him.

I came across the second example as I scrolled down my Facebook page. Someone had posted a picture of a group of protesters (anarchists) in black garb with a skinny, young white dude front and center in a t-shirt featuring a stick-man tossing a cross into a trashcan. The caption read, "If Jesus comes back, we'll kill him again." As much as this appalled me, God gave me the grace to avoid a hateful, knee-jerk reaction. I pondered the poor man's plight. Obviously, he didn't realize that on the last day of this earth's history, he and everyone else would bend the knee and confess Jesus as Lord. I earnestly hoped that he would hear the word and repent before it was too late. In sincerity I prayed that he would hear the sweet gospel message that Christ died for all so that no one would have to go to hell.

President Trump announced his Fake News Awards and CNN garnered the most "wins" in the list of top ten doozies. NYT writer Paul Krugman secured the top spot with his election-night prediction that the stock market would crash and never recover. Deplorables belly-laughed and noted how the DOW had skyrocketed eight-thousand points since then.

1/19/18: The media droned on and on about the looming midnight government shutdown; yawn. Dems and Republicans pointed the fingers at each other but the latter seemed to make a stronger case since the House Republicans passed a one-month continuing resolution the night before and Democrats controlled the outcome in the Senate where passage required sixty votes. For his part,

President Trump invited Chuck Schumer to the White House to try to avert a shutdown. To Deplorables, the bottom line appeared to be that Democrats would fight tooth and nail to benefit illegal immigrants at the expense of American citizens.

The House bill garnered a few Democrat votes since the GOP sweetened the pot for them by extending child healthcare spending by six years. Nancy Pelosi put things in perspective by comparing the child healthcare add-on to a cherry on top of a "doggie doo-doo" sundae. Wow, first she called $1,000-$3,000 bonuses **"crumbs"** and now turned up her nose at healthcare coverage for children and compared it to Fido's feces. Deplorables thought this was the height of hypocrisy for her to publicly bring the topic of excrement into play. Hadn't the Dems just spent the past week in hysterics over the President's supposed use of the S-word in a private setting?

It had been forty-five years since Roe v. Wade legalized the murder of babies in America. Since then, the March for Life had gathered in D. C.

annually to support the right to life. Never had a sitting U. S. President addressed the marchers. That was, until Donald Trump made another historic break from the past. President Trump left the White House to personally address the crowd there and broadcast his speech via satellite so that the tens of thousands at the Washington Mall and elsewhere could witness his remarks live. It lifted the spirits of Deplorables everywhere to see the President boldly stand up for our most cherished right: the right to life.

1/20/18: This was the anniversary of President Trump's inauguration. Deplorables toasted the Commander-in-Chief for a remarkable first year that included a host of truly noteworthy accomplishments. He saved the Supreme Court with the confirmation of Justice Neil Gorsuch. President Trump unleashed the shackled economy and showered Americans with trillions in new wealth generated by the startling turnaround and record-breaking stock market. He pushed through the first major tax cuts and reforms in thirty years. The Businessman-in-Chief demolished a mountain of stifling regulations President Obama had imposed and boosted consumer and business confidence into the stratosphere.

He stood up for religious freedom and valiantly jousted with the corrupt, evil, lying media and withstood a barrage of attempts to undermine his presidency through the Russia hoax and other subterfuge. The President ended the unjust individual healthcare mandate that unfairly penalized so many Americans. He opened up ANWR and launched America toward energy independence. Showing true, bold leadership, President Trump restored America's standing in the world and demolished ISIS's caliphate with the help of our allies. He recognized Jerusalem as Israel's capital and put our enemies on notice in the Palestinian Authority, Pakistan, Russia, China, Iran and North Korea.

President Trump fulfilled his role as a true Washington outsider. He worked tirelessly to implement his agenda by keeping his campaign promises. President Trump proved to be a man of honor and his word. So how did the Dems show their appreciation? They crashed the party and dropped a *Baby Ruth* in the punch bowl by shutting down the government. The Dems in the Senate stabbed the American people in the back in order to deny President Trump.

This time it appeared they badly miscalculated because even many liberals saw through their lies and put the blame for the Schumer Shutdown on the Dems. The Republicans in the House had passed a clean CR that contained nothing objectionable to the Dems. Yet the Dems voted it down by injecting a wholly unrelated issue into the mix: DACA. Deplorables and most Americans would not soon forget how Schumer and his minions had screwed them over in favor of illegal immigrants. Even as polls showed they'd shot themselves in the foot, they doubled down and said they also needed billions to bail out union pensions before they'd release the government from the hostage situation they'd created. **Why did the Democrats refer to American citizens as Deplorables but illegal immigrants as Dreamers?**

So called women's marches took place around the country. I wouldn't initiate your gag reflex by recounting the vulgar costumes and signs displayed by some. Suffice it to say that a lot of loony tunes came out to play. It wasn't really about women. More than anything else, it was a Trump hate-fest intended to cast a pall over the anniversary of the President's inauguration. Conservative women weren't welcome. This march reflected the polar opposite of all the women who joined in on the March for Life. By the way, what did they mean by "women's rights" anyway? Didn't all Americans have the same rights regardless of race, gender, religion, etc.?

1/22/18: The Little Cobra ... that's how I came to think of "Crying, Lying, A-Shutdown-is-What-I-be-Trying" Chuck Schumer in honor of The Rip Cords and their classic song *Hey Little Cobra* (don't you know you're gonna shut 'em down) ... got into a staring contest with President Trump and blinked. That's because the American people saw through his lies and realized he had put the rights of illegal immigrants ahead of those of citizens. He caved and directed his Democrat brothers in the Senate to approve another short-term CR through February 8th. President Trump proved to be the adult in the room by refusing to negotiate on DACA while "Shutdown Schumer" tried to hold the American public and military hostage. So all Chucky accomplished was to waste three days in order to play kick-the-can again.

While everyone concentrated on the shutdown sideshow, only FNC reported on the real, earth-shattering news about Deep State corruption in the FBI. More evidence surfaced of a massive cover-up that made Nixon's Watergate crew seem like a JV team. As investigators neared pay dirt, the FBI claimed that they'd lost five months of text messages between illicit lovebirds Peter Strzok and Lisa Page from December 14 through May 17, 2017. They offered some lame, convoluted excuse about the two FBI agent's Samsung 5 phones malfunctioning. It just so happened that the problem got fixed on May 17 when Robert Mueller was appointed as Special Counsel. ABC, CBS and NBC didn't give this groundbreaking story a minute of coverage, not a single second!

Other curiosities surfaced that made the whole thing stink to high heaven. Apparently, AG Loretta Lynch of the Bill Clinton tarmac meeting fame knew before Hillary Clinton was even interviewed that she'd be exonerated in the email investigation. This conflicted with James Comey's testimony before Congress. One of the texts between Strzok and Page that wasn't magically lost contained a reference to a "secret society" within the FBI dedicated to bringing down President Trump.

Still, the Dems and the Deep State persisted with the cover-up. While the majority of Republicans in Congress had read the four-page Foreign Intelligence Surveillance Act (FISA) memo summarizing the corruption afoot in the DOJ and FBI, only one Dem took the time. The public clamored to have the memo declassified so we could judge for ourselves but the ranking minority member on the Intelligence Committee, Rep. Adam Schiff, argued against it. Deplorables wanted to know where in the hell were AG Jeff Sessions and FBI Director Christopher Wray? And why was the latter so beholden to shamed Deputy Director Andrew McCabe?

1/24/18: Democrats continued to flaunt their disdain for freedom of speech. UConn barred the public from attending a speech by conservative Ben Shapiro for fear of offending fragile snowflakes. Some of America's Democrat Mayors took a lesson from the Dems in Congress who threatened to boycott the State of the Union Address and bypassed the chance to meet with President Trump. Leading the charge was NYC Mayor Bill DeBlasio who cut off his nose to spite his face rather than engaging the President in an open dialogue about sanctuary cities.

As the President prepared to depart for Davos, Switzerland to attend the World Economic Forum, the Press floated rumors that some leaders of African nations would boycott President Trump's speech to show their displeasure with his supposed blank-hole comments.

Deplorables clearly saw the truth behind such childish behavior. Liberals loathed free speech and refused to share a conversation with the other side because it would expose the lunacy of their positions. Inside of their group-think bubbles, their idiocy appeared quite normal since they didn't allow for any competing standards of sanity. But when ideas were allowed to flow freely and compete on equal footing in an open forum, their mental illnesses were exposed.

President Trump went about the business of the American people like an adult. He listened to the mayors who attended his forum but made it clear that he supported the DOJ's crackdown on illegal immigration and would withhold federal monies from cities that openly defied federal law. He showed compassion for so called Dreamers, even hinting at a possible path toward citizenship, but stood firm on achieving border security and immigration reform that would solve the problem permanently.

As for the rumored African boycott, the President didn't take it personally but instead set up a meeting with Rwandan President Paul Kagame who also served as Chair of the African Union. Deplorables hoped the President would employ his personal charm and statesmanship to win over President Kagame who might in turn positively influence African Union leaders prior to his speech.

Stunningly, rumors leaked that former FBI Director James Comey had hired Daniel Richman to be his attorney. Comey had famously leaked classified FBI records to the Press through his law professor pal Richman. Comey admitted that he did so in order to prompt the hiring of a Special Counsel to investigate the Russian collusion hoax. Deplorables asked *why Comey would do this*. Ah yes, this would create an attorney-client privilege between Comey and Richman and thus help to shield Comey from the mounting list of questions from congressional investigators.

Comey revealed his true nature one day prior when he quoted this from Martin Luther King, Jr., "The ultimate measure of a man is not where he stands in moments of comfort and convenience, but where he stands at times of challenge and controversy." This sounded noble but really did a disservice to the great civil rights leader since it was taken so horribly out of context. This is what Deplorables heard through the filter of common sense and truth. Comey, like many far-left ideologues, adhered to Saul Alinsky's *Rules for Radicals* and the number one precept that the ends justified the means.

He cleverly tried to justify his criminal, possibly treasonous and certainly unethical behavior by painting himself as a martyr and self-appointed freedom fighter.

President Trump made Deplorables including me very nervous by telling reporters he would welcome the opportunity to speak to Special Counsel Robert Mueller, even under oath. We could admire the President for being willing to back up his steadfast claim that there was no collusion or obstruction but worried that he didn't recognize the jeopardy involved.

Deplorables knew that the truth didn't matter. We believed that Robert Mueller would go to any lengths, including sophistry and even outright lying, to bring down the President. We could only hope that President Trump's lawyers would protect him from Mueller's perjury trap. The Special Counsel's track record with Manafort, Flynn and Papodopoulos showed how far he would stray from Russian collusion to collect scalps. Of course he would employ trickery to try to claim the biggest trophy of all. Deplorables still laughed derisively at the ironic notion of anyone being charged with lying to the shameless liars in the FBI and DOJ.

Former Secretary of State John Kerry reportedly met with Hussein Agha, a close associate of Palestinian Authority President Mahmoud Abbas, in London. According to reports, Kerry told Agha to pass along to Abbas that he should "hold on and be strong." Kerry also supposedly encouraged Abbas to be patient because he speculated that President Trump wouldn't be in office much longer. Deplorables wondered if Kerry would be charged under the Logan Act. Sources also said the Ketchup King (by marriage) hinted that he would run for president.

The Logan Act of 1799 was designed to stop U. S. citizens from contacting foreign agents to influence a foreign government's policies in disputes with the United States. Although no one had ever been prosecuted under the Logan Act, desperate Dems had pulled it out of mothballs to try to go after Michael Flynn and Jared Kushner as part of the Russia hoax. Would they now go after Kerry who allegedly went on foreign soil to intervene directly against a sitting President's peace plan for the Middle East?

Deplorables guessed no, that the double standard would be applied yet again for a Dem who had betrayed his country before when, as a young Navy veteran, Kerry appeared at congressional hearings in 1971 to protest the Vietnam War in which he'd served. It was neither heroic nor patriotic. He showed his true colors when he lied about atrocities and threw away the medals he'd earned in combat.

1/25/18: I hadn't paid attention to polls since the 2016 election when they proved to be astoundingly unreliable but this one caught my eye. It asked whether the economy had improved under President Trump. Surprisingly, in spite of the negative coverage from the Press, forty percent of respondents said the economy was better under President Trump. Of the remainder, thirty-four percent said it remained the same and twenty-two percent said things had gotten worse.

Deplorables shook their heads and tried to fathom how those twenty-two percent could see a poorer economy with unemployment way down, salaries up, bonuses flowing, consumer confidence soaring and a stock market that had skyrocketed over forty percent since the inauguration. Still, the forty percent favorable respondents showed that the truth was sinking in where it counted; in people's wallets. Another poll the same day showed the President's approval rating up from thirty-eight to forty-five percent. It still seemed depressed but appeared to reflect the true mood of the people trending up.

Low and behold, the IG said he'd found some of the perhaps fifty-thousand missing texts exchanged between Peter Strzok and Lisa Page during the critical period between the presidential election and appointment of the Special Counsel. I guessed that the outcry from conservative members of Congress and the American people convinced someone to try to assuage the masses. This only incensed Deplorables further. What did they mean by some? Who in the hell was controlling which texts were found or lost?

President Trump put out a detailed proposal for a DACA fix. He showed his compassion and willingness to compromise. The President didn't change his demand for a southern border wall but loosened his stand on ending chain migration by allowing parents into the mix. The President's proposal increased the DACA population from about seven-hundred-thousand to roughly 1.8 million. He even went so far as to risk alienating his base by hinting at a ten-to-twelve-year path to citizenship or, in conservative parlance, amnesty. How did the Left react to this incredible olive branch? They labeled the President's offer as a white supremacist plan. This showed that liberals didn't really want a DACA solution if it meant a win for President Trump or they were mentally ill ... or both.

1/26/18: President Trump addressed the crowd at the World Economic Forum in Davos, Switzerland. The audience seemed captivated and apparently no one followed through with the threatened walkout. Deplorables and, frankly, many others including even some opponents found President Trump's speech to be incredibly refreshing and liberating after eight years of the Obama apology tour.

The President didn't make excuses but proudly proclaimed he represented America first. He made the case that a strong America, leading from the front rather than behind, was good for the entire world. He touted America's successes and promised more to come. Our Salesman-in-Chief declared America to be open for business and invited the world to join us. He didn't back down on trade but called for free and open trade based on fairness and reciprocity.

Not once did he mention the grandest hoax and rallying cry of the globalists: climate change. While in Davos, the President hosted a dinner with fifteen of the world's most important business leaders. He also took time to sit down with key allies like Theresa May and Benjamin Netanyahu. Deplorables sighed, ah … finally a business-savvy, patriotic leader rather than the world's doormat.

The media had to find an excuse to ignore the big, positive news out of Davos so they concocted another fake news story. Led by the failing New York Times, headlines screamed that President Trump had tried to fire Special Counsel Robert Mueller. According to the loony, liberal haters in the Press, this amounted to obstruction of justice. However, President Trump denied the story. So Deplorables had a choice of believing the President or more anonymous sources quoted by the NYT.

Deplorables assumed that, of course, President Trump had at least considered the option of canning Mueller and ending the witch hunt. Amidst the hubbub, one fact stood in the way of this latest obstruction hoax gaining traction: Robert Mueller hadn't been fired. Deplorables had to laugh, or cry, at the hypocrisy of these claims coming from the Left as they worked feverishly to cover up actual obstruction by the Obama-politicized FBI and DOJ.

Deplorables could always look to the land of fruits and nuts for comic relief and the California legislature came through with flying colors. They introduced a bill that would make it illegal for waiters to offer straws to customers that hadn't asked for them. Actually, it was kind of scary to think that, with all the major problems they faced, California Dems put drinking straws at the top of the list.

Apparently, some sane people still resided in the big blue state. A group of conservative Californians (oxymoron?) proposed splitting the state in two with the coast being separate from the rest. Deplorables guffawed at the geographical significance of such a sober proposition: the coastline appeared to be, literally and figuratively, the farthest Left place in America. If the split ever passed, Deplorables wondered if the border wall would run north and south between the coastal region and the rest of California.

Deplorables got another dose of truth-is-stranger-than-fiction when reports surfaced that a senior advisor to Hillary Clinton in her 2008 campaign, Burns Strider, had been accused of sexual harassment. The campaign retained Strider, allegedly at Hillary's request, even after the accusations were made known. Deplorables shook their heads once again at the deliciously absurd hypocrisy of this self-appointed champion of women harboring another sexual predator, that is, other than her husband. That the New York Times produced this story showed how far out of favor Hillary had fallen with the Left.

Nancy Pelosi provided more jaw-dropping comments. She doubled down on her **crumbs** comment and called $1,000 - $3,000 bonuses small as compared to the "bonanza" reaped by the corporations. Then she took to the podium for more bombast and said President Trump's overly generous DACA offer was an attempt to make America white again. Did the Dems have anything other than identity politics and the race card? Debbie Wasserman Schultz came to Pelosi's defense and also labeled $1,000 bonuses as **crumbs** and then pointed out that they wouldn't be $1,000 because they'd be taxed. Yes folks, she actually criticized the bonuses resulting from tax cuts because they'd be taxed!

1/27/18: Deplorables were treated to celebrity bombast over the weekend prior to the SOTU Address ... as if they needed more. Chelsea Handler (Did she still qualify as a celebrity?) pinpointed white women as being the most Deplorable by denouncing the majority of fifty-three percent that voted for Donald Trump. Didn't those women know that they were supposed to vote as a block for Crooked Hillary because of their lady parts?

Jay Z chimed in and hurled pejoratives at the President and claimed he was out of touch with people in the inner cities. Hello, McFly ... had you been living in a cave or did it just appear so because you'd gotten all of your news from CNN or the NYT? President Trump was in the process of making good on his promise to minorities stuck in Democrat-controlled urban centers. Unemployment was down to historic levels among blacks and Hispanics. Everyone stood to gain from the tax cuts. The booming economy offered hope and opportunity to people stuck in Democrat strongholds. And the President still aimed to provide inner city kids and their parents with school choices. I assumed that Jay Z must have been the black version of Nancy Pelosi … so rich and out of touch with real folks that he couldn't tell **crumbs** from real blessings.

Peter Maas wrote an article titled *It's Time to Wage War Against War Movies That Glorify Outdated Models of Masculinity*. He took to task the recent release of *12 Strong*, a true story about a Special Forces team that fought the Taliban in Afghanistan after 9/11. According to folks like Maas, we needed to divorce ourselves from toxic masculinity. Did that mean we needed to use unisex bathrooms? Deplorables decided instead that we needed to halt the wussification of America.

1/28/18: Like most Deplorables, I didn't bother
watching the Grammy's but couldn't avoid the news
coverage. Predictably, it quickly descended into an
anti-Trump political rally. I was able to sum up the
whole hate-spewing spectacle in this one capsule.
None other than Hillary Clinton showed up to read
an excerpt from Michael Wolff's book of lies, *Fire
and Fury*. Actually, it made perfect sense to have a
pathological liar read from a discredited, trashy
tabloid book full of unsubstantiated poppycock.
However, it made no sense to thrust Loser Hillary in
front of the public again. Deplorables still wondered
if she would ever go away.

1/29/18: A conservative group called Campus
Reform posted a hilarious video of a young man
interviewing NYU students about the President's
SOTU Address. To a person, they decried the speech
and basically expressed their hatred for anything
related to Donald Trump. There was only one
problem. President Trump hadn't delivered the
speech yet! It didn't matter because their tiny,
closed minds were already made up. Some went so
far as to comment on parts of the imaginary address
they hadn't heard. One noted some racist comments

and another even referred to a chant supposedly led by the President. Although comical, this captured the sad state of affairs on American campuses.

News outlets reported the tragic news that twenty-five-year-old Detroit police officer Glenn Doss, Jr. died. The young, African-American man had been shot the week prior while responding to a domestic violence call. Predictably, we didn't hear any outrage from Black Lives Matter, Al Sharpton or Jesse Jackson. Deplorables surmised that Doss's black life apparently didn't matter to BLM since he served as a police officer and his killer was also black. Again, the Dems failed to bring up gun control since they didn't sympathize with the victim.

A video went viral showing an El Rancho, CA High School teacher, Gregory Salcido, demeaning U. S. Military members in an expletive-laced, classroom rant. Thankfully, we gained insight into this disgusting display through a courageous student who recorded his teacher's diatribe on his phone. Salcido claimed that people who served in the military were intellectual lightweights who couldn't cut it in academia. Yes, he basically called our selfless defenders of freedom a bunch of Deplorables. When asked about Salcido a day later, the White House Chief of Staff, General John Kelly, summed things up well for Deplorables when he said the traitorous teacher could go to hell.

There was good news for those who preferred being spoon fed political pabulum instead of hearing things straight from the horse's mouth. The former was soothing and safe while the latter required some rigor: thinking and making up one's own mind. A group of Hollywood elites including Mark Ruffalo and Whoopie Goldberg announced plans to stage a People's State of the Union Address for those too sensitive to watch the real thing. This took fake news and anti-Trumpism to a whole new level.

That loud noise we heard was the first shoe dropping. The Deputy Director of the FBI, Andrew McCabe, "stepped down" from his post. Deplorables asked two questions: 1) *who would be next and* 2) *were they really going to let this guy walk away with his pension?*

1/30/18: President Trump rose to the occasion and knocked it out park in delivering his first State of the Union Address. He struck a serious but positive tone … some might say presidential … in declaring the state of the union strong because the American people were strong. The President maintained this wonderful theme throughout his speech, not dwelling on himself or his accomplishments but the people. He addressed all of the people, not just conservatives or Republicans. All in all, it was a rousing, uplifting speech that could have made Ronald Reagan proud.

President Trump didn't pander but stayed the course in his crusade to make America great again. However, he did it in a way that reached out to both sides of the aisle and to every corner of our nation.

The President was incredibly effective in putting the spotlight where it belonged, on everyday Americans from vastly different walks of life. He shared their tragic, exhilarating and uplifting stories in a way that made spirits soar. Sibling small business owners, Steve Staub and Sandy Keplinger of Dayton, OH and one of their employees, Corey Adams, exulted in the opportunity to show how the President's policies had turned their fortunes around. The President feted a young boy, Preston Sharp, who took it upon himself to see that the graves of forty-thousand veterans were festooned with American flags and carnations. A young police officer from Albuquerque, Ryan Holets, and his wife, parents with their own children, brought the baby they'd adopted to help a hopeless mother struggling with opioid addiction.

Love and compassion was showered upon two couples whose daughters were killed by MS-13 gang members. Honor was bestowed upon a young combat veteran, Army Staff Sergeant Justin Pack, who braved a booby trapped house to save the life of a fellow soldier who'd just been blown up. The President recognized another man, Corporal Matthew Bradford, who'd lost both legs and his sight in combat only to survive and re-enlist in the Marines. We met and heard the story of a young, female Coast Guard member, Ashlee Leppert, who had risked her life to save the lives of some forty hurricane victims. We also became acquainted with David Dahlberg, a fire prevention technician who saved sixty-two people from the massive California wildfires.

The most heart-rending story involved North Korean defector Ji Seong Ho. Facing starvation under Kim Jong-un's brutal dictatorship, he tried to steal some coal to barter for food but became so weak that he collapsed on some train tracks and lost a leg and hand when it ran over him. His siblings literally ate dirt and had their growth stunted in order to share what little food they had to nurse their injured brother back to health. When Ji Seong Ho recovered, Kim's thugs tortured the amputee and demanded to know if he'd come across any Christians in China.

He had encountered some Christians and they helped to motivate him to persevere and seek freedom. He hobbled across Southeast Asia to escape and his poor father was consequently tortured to death back in North Korea. When the President joyfully proclaimed that Ji Seong Ho now lived in South Korea and helped other defectors to seek freedom, the proud young man stood on his prosthetic leg and joyously raised his now unnecessary crutches into the air.

While the President didn't back away from his campaign pledges to the American people, he still tried to offer several olive branches to the Democrats.

Nothing demonstrated his unique ability to stand on principle while simultaneously reaching across the aisle better than his comments on immigration. In one breath he outlined a compromise that offered a pathway to citizenship for not just the seven-hundred-thousand Obama DACA recipients but almost tripled that number at 1.8 million. At the same time, he thrilled his base and most reasonable independents by declaring that Americans were Dreamers too.

The reaction of the Democrats stunned onlookers, even in these highly fractured, hyper-partisan times. The dour Dems sat on their hands for almost the entire duration. Of course, the party out of power always sat for parts of past SOTU Addresses when certain policy differences arose. But throughout our long history, there had always been numerous comments that brought nearly unanimous approval despite party lines. The distraught, desperate Dems blew that laudable precedent to smithereens. Close up shots of Nancy Pelosi and Chuck Schumer seemed to reflect much more than disappointment or even extreme disapproval; they glowered with disgust and utter hatred. They couldn't even stand up for the little boy,

Preston Sharp, who showed such amazing patriotism and support for our veterans.

Here was a list of talking points that the Dems couldn't support. A booming stock market that added $8 trillion in wealth to America and helped the 401Ks and pension plans of millions of people to skyrocket warranted not even a smile. Economic growth, job growth, burgeoning consumer confidence and tax cuts went over like lead balloons amongst the Dems. Surely they applauded the astounding defeat of ISIS, right? Nope and there didn't appear to be an ounce of patriotism in the Dems when the President mentioned our Anthem, American Flag and proper care for our veterans. Even feel-good topics fell flat with the pouting politicians on the Left: the American dream, unifying America, battling drug addiction, curbing crime, making government accountable, lowering prescription drug costs and discovering new, life-saving medicines.

In one of the more shocking displays, the members of the Democrat Black Caucus sat and scowled as President Trump proudly announced that black unemployment had dropped to an all-time low.

269

Were they really in favor of high unemployment among African-Americans? Perhaps they were just in a bad mood about polls that showed more black voters shifting allegiances based on results versus rhetoric. One black Congressman in the middle of the caucus had the nerve to smile and clap but tried to hide his appreciation. That's because Nancy Pelosi stood and turned backward several times to scold any Dem that dared to applaud anything the President said.

Representative Luis Gutierrez, an America-hating traitor from Illinois, actually walked out of the hall before the President finished his speech, right in the midst of "USA" chants. But even that couldn't top what happened earlier when President Trump played his ace in the hole. He proclaimed our national motto: In God We Trust. Speaker Paul Ryan simultaneously pointed to the same words inscribed in stone above the rostrum. What did the petulant Dems do? They remained seated and mute and figuratively turned their backs on God. I said this earlier and believed it but this really made it sink in as the cameras spanned the hall and showed the Democrat side of the aisle disrespecting God. No, this wasn't your grandfather's Democrat Party any more. They shunned God in the middle of a nationally televised SOTU Address. How could President Trump and the Republicans hope for a compromise on anything? There could be no compromise between good and evil.

As if the Dem's childish attempts at resistance during the SOTU Address weren't enough, they foisted wet-behind-the-ears Joseph Kennedy III to deliver one of their several disjointed responses. It looked like they'd pulled Richie Cunningham into Fonzie's car repair garage to give a campaign speech to become student council president. Deplorables snickered at the sight of a Kennedy standing by a wrecked car and wondered if anyone else remembered Ted Kennedy's most cowardly hour when he left Mary Jo Kopechne to die in the waters near Chappaquiddick Island. To make matters worse for the freckle-faced lad, he had applied so much Chap Stick to his mouth that it made it look like he was drooling. Maybe he wanted to mimic Nancy Pelosi.

Kennedy the water carrier didn't say anything substantive about the policy issues because the Dems had no platform. He immediately launched into name calling and played the race card. Kennedy must have learned well from Pelosi and Schumer that if you didn't have anything else to say you should just scream racist at the top of your lungs. I listened long enough to see that he intended to employ the same tired, divisive rhetoric through identity politics: race, gender, etc. For good measure, he threw in class warfare and decried CEOs for making so much more than entry-level employees ... yawn. Deplorables wondered if this "expert" had ever run a business or done an honest day's work in his life.

1/31/18: The media did their best to put a negative spin on things but sane people had eyes and couldn't be swayed from the masterpiece they'd witnessed. The loony, liberal Press speculated whether there might have been a hidden meaning in First Lady Melania Trump's choice of a white pants suit. Then they piled on further and questioned why she rode to the Capital Building separately from the President. Deplorables screamed *she showed courtesy, compassion and class by accompanying her many guests*!

Crazy Maxine Watters who didn't even attend the SOTU Address held a press conference to call the

President a racist again. Members of the Black Caucus called for impeachment proceedings again. The libs downplayed MS-13 as if mentioning them was an affront to people of color (by the way, white is a skin color too). This was like President Obama when he called ISIS the JV team. MS-13 had seven-thousand members across the U. S. who had committed dozens of horrific murders!

The media excoriated the President for not mentioning Russia. Really ... did they complain that President Obama hadn't used his SOTU Addresses to dwell on Fast and Furious, Benghazi, the IRS debacle or any of the host of other scandals that dogged him? In using this absurd argument, the media had to lie again because President Trump did mention Russia ... as an adversary along with China, North Korea and Iran.

Everyone expected that the media would drop some kind of old bombshell to change the narrative away from the President's successful SOTU Address. However, no one anticipated a literal train wreck would aid them in their quest to derail the President's agenda. For the first half of the day, the good news flowed freely. Then word came that the Amtrak train carrying some two-hundred GOP members of Congress and their families had struck a large truck on the track near Charlottesville, VA. They had been headed to the Greenbrier in West Virginia for their annual policy-making retreat. One person in the truck was killed and several other people were injured.

Just like that, the media had their excuse to ignore the SOTU Address and slow down the President's momentum. Deplorables didn't want to think anyone had sunk that low but couldn't help wondering if the accident hadn't been planned. While that appeared unlikely, it raised questions about our nation's government-run passenger railway. Had big government liberals received a political windfall as a result of another glaring failure by one of their state-run businesses? Only time would tell. In the meantime, the Republicans showed real grit and determination by still making their way to the Greenbrier by bus in order to conduct the important work of the American people.

Like Jason Chaffetz before him, Rep. Trey Gowdy succumbed to the urge to extricate himself from the swamp and announced he would retire from Congress. We couldn't blame him but Deplorables mourned the loss of another good man in leadership and the sad state of affairs in our nation's capital. It would take investigators weeks to determine what happened to that Amtrak train carrying most of the GOP members of Congress but one thing became clear immediately. Numerous TDS-infected, insane liberals took to Twitter to thank God (the god they didn't believe in) for driving out Trey Gowdy and … yes … wrecking the train carrying GOP members of Congress. Surely they knew that spouses and children were on board and that at least one person had died. It didn't matter because their blind hatred showed.

2/1/18: Polls showed that ninety-seven percent of Republicans, seventy-two percent of Independents and even forty-three percent of Democrats viewed the President's SOTU Address favorably. Would Chuck Schumer, Nancy Pelosi and their fellow Democrat politicians ever learn? Apparently they wouldn't since they continued their scorched earth resistance movement unabated. As the President moved toward release of the FISA memo approved earlier by the Intelligence Committee, the Dems lit their hair on fire in an attempt to quash any transparency. They called it an attack on the FBI and DOJ and evil Adam Schiff even tried to discredit it by saying the Republicans materially altered the document. Democrats evoked bad memories of Joseph McCarthy with their coercive attempts to cover up the truth. They vowed to issue their own memo; their own version of the truth. Their moral relativism reminded Deplorables of Pontius Pilate washing his hands.

A steady stream of companies, this time Lowe's, announced more $1,000 bonuses for employees. Corporations heralded plans to bring manufacturing and investments back to the USA just as President Trump had promised. For example, Apple announced plans to invest $350 billion and create twenty-thousand new jobs in America and … wonder of wonders … Chrysler said they would bring car production from Mexico back to Michigan. The tax breaks that Nancy Pelosi called **"crumbs"** started to kick in. My oldest son happily informed me that his wife had just received a bump of over two percent in her paycheck thanks to the change in withholding.

2/2/18: The President signed off and Congress released the much disputed FISA memo from the Intelligence Committee. It showed two things clearly. First, the Obama Administration's DOJ and FBI were politicized and weaponized to spy on the opposing party's presidential campaign. They used opposition research from the Clinton campaign to secure the FISA warrant under false pretenses. Deputy FBI Director Andrew McCabe admitted that they never would have obtained the FISA warrant without the fake Fusion GPS dossier and, thus, the Mueller Russian collusion investigation never would have been initiated. The memo showed that the British spy behind the fake dossier, Christopher Steele, was openly anti-Trump. He had leaked fake news to Yahoo that was in turn used to corroborate the dossier to the FISA court. The judge wasn't aware of the circular logic used to pull the wool over his eyes.

Secondly, the memo contained nothing even remotely sensitive or classified in regard to national security. It said nothing about sources or methods of intelligence that would put anyone in danger. The memo only exposed bad actors within the FBI and DOJ. All the hand wringing and clamoring by the

Dems, DOJ and FBI about the release of the memo were a bald-faced lie and attempted cover-up. The Dems didn't quit though. They worked feverishly to issue their own memo, their own version of the truth, to try to muddy the waters. Deplorables demanded that Christopher Wray be fired and Rosenstein, Comey, Lynch, Clinton, Strzok, Page, Weissmann and perhaps Obama be put behind bars. Deplorables also wanted to see Robert Mueller fined the same amount that taxpayers had been forced to squander on his contrived investigation.

Part Four: Unfinished Business

"Americans are Dreamers too." (President Donald J. Trump during his 1st SOTU Address on 1/30/18)

This was indeed the wildest ride of any President's first year in office. Deplorables and all Americans had every reason to celebrate after a year of phenomenal accomplishments. America had made a turn for the better and seemed to be on the right track again. We could be optimistic and even proud. Yet, the bulk of the work in making America great again remained unfinished and significant dangers abounded. Deplorables asked *where we should go from here.*

My first advice is don't rest on your Deplorable laurels. The resistance is intractable so we must remain vigilant. I've chronicled the first year in detail for everyone but that's not the end of the story. Stay on top of the news and keep notes if necessary. As shown herein, we're in uncharted waters and it takes some work to keep track of the sheer lunacy of the Left. They remain committed to overthrowing the President that we the people duly elected. As we've seen, they will stop at nothing to accomplish their mission.

Keep in mind what our end goal is here. We need to maintain our Deplorable majority in the House and overcome our minority status in the Senate. Don't be fooled by the fifty-one to forty-nine Republican edge that supposedly exists in the Senate. The Democrats currently have the majority with the help of RINOs Susan Collins, John McCain, Jeff Flake, Bob Corker, Lamar Alexander, Shelley Moore Capito, Dean Heller, Rob Portman and Lisa Murkowski.

Thankfully, Jeff Flake and Bob Corker have already taken themselves out and sadly John McCain has more serious matters to tend to with his health issues. As for the others, don't be swayed by their willingness to support the tax cuts. Just remember that they abandoned us when push came to shove on Obamacare. Unfortunately, we can only fix three of these problems in 2018 by replacing Jeff Flake (AZ), Bob Corker (TN) and Dean Heller (NV) with true conservatives. We can only wish and pray for the best for John McCain (AZ) and seek a strong conservative replacement as necessary.

The good news is that there are only five other GOP Senate seats up in 2018 and Ted Cruz (TX), John Barrasso (WY), Deb Fischer (NE), and Roger Wicker (MS) deserve our support for re-election. The grand old man, Orrin Hatch (UT) is retiring so it will be important to find a suitable replacement. Please, please good voters of Utah do not go blue by electing Trump-hating, super-RINO Mitt Romney. A leopard doesn't change its spots. Do your homework and find a Deplorable Senate candidate who truly supports the President's agenda to make America great again. A litmus test should be whether they will actively advocate for tough but fair immigration reform. Don't be influenced by President Trump's endorsement of Mitt Romney.

The even better news is that the Senate Democrats must defend twenty-six seats if you include two Independents who are definitely not conservative:

Bernie Sanders (VT) and Angus King (ME). We should try to oust every last one of these Democrat Senators. It will be tough since some of them reside in solidly blue states but there is hope. Deplorables aren't alone in this fight. The vast majority of Independents are leaning conservative on important issues like immigration reform, the economy and national security. Even a good number of Democrat voters were shocked by the disgusting display of their leaders at the SOTU Address against the flag, veterans, fair trade, border security and undeniable economic success including low unemployment among blacks and Hispanics.

Here's the list of seats that need to be turned over to gain a majority in the Senate and keep America on the right track: Dianne Feinstein (CA), Chris Murphy (CT), Tom Carper (DE), Bill Nelson (FL), Mazie Hirono (HI), Joe Donnelly (IN) [Rep. Todd Rokita would be a great replacement], Angus King (ME), Ben Cardin (MD), Elizabeth "Pocahontas" Warren (MS), Debbie Stabenow (MI), Amy Klobuchar (MN), Tina Smith (MN), Claire McCaskill (MO), Jon Tester (MT), Bob "Hung Jury" Menendez (NJ), Martin Heinrich (NM), Kirsten Gillibrand (NY), Heidi Heitkamp (ND), Sherrod Brown (OH), Bob Casey Jr. (PA), Sheldon Whitehouse (RI), Bernie Sanders (VT), Tim Kaine (VA), Maria Cantwell (WA), Joe Manchin (WV) and Tammy Baldwin (WI).

I can almost hear some of you complaining out there. *How can you summarily dismiss the whole group based on party affiliation*? Remember, this is not about partisan politics. It's not even about liberalism versus conservatism. The Democrats are no longer the party of John Kennedy or anything close to it. Liberalism no longer embraces the ideals of freedom and liberty. Today's brand of liberalism has been infected by TDS; a mental illness characterized by blind hatred and an end-justifies-the-means mentality. They support fascists (Anti-Fa) and anarchists (Occupy and BLM) who use violence and coercion to shut down free speech. They've declared open war on the police and support open borders and globalism over the interests and values of the American people. Many of you would have labeled me as crazy a short time ago for seeing today's stark political divide as a battle between good and evil. That is, until you saw the scowling faces of Democrats at the SOTU Address as they hissed when the President mentioned some of our most cherished ideals.

Let's single out a couple of Senators to drive my point home. In my state of Missouri, Claire McCaskill has been moving toward the center at the eleventh hour in an attempt to hold onto power. We will not be fooled. If re-elected, she will resist the President and the American people every step of the way as we work to make America great again. My fellow Missourians please remember this if nothing else. Claire McCaskill is a charter member of the culture of death having the blood of countless aborted babies on her hands. Joe Manchin is the poster boy for "moderate" Democrats. Surely, he should be spared, right? No way, not unless you can show me one time that he voted yes on any of President Trump's significant MAGA proposals. That goes for this whole list of Senators. Just remember, not a one of them voted for the tax cuts. Instead, they all lied and said they were tax cuts for the rich. Then they compounded their mendacity by referring to your $1,000 - $3,000 bonuses and tax cuts as **"crumbs."**

There are too many House seats up for grabs in 2018 to name them all but it is crucial that conservatives maintain the edge here. The only way to make America great again is to keep the House in Republican hands while delivering a true sixty-vote majority in the Senate. Are you encouraged by the astounding economic turnaround that has occurred since President Trump started slashing foolish, anti-business regulations and led the charge on tax cuts and reforms? Everyone knows that there's normally a natural backlash against the party in power during the first mid-term after a new president is elected but would that make any sense? If you want to continue to see improvements in prosperity, security and America's standing in the world, then the same logic has to apply in the House. We need to oust Democrats and RINOs at every chance. Even folks that may not like President Trump from a personal standpoint should acknowledge the results he has achieved and clamor for more.

Besides following the news in general, what should we do to prepare ourselves for the 2018 mid-terms? First, pay attention and get involved in the primaries. Half of the battle is getting good candidates on the ballot. Don't let the Republicans in your state and district put up RINOs who don't support our MAGA agenda. After you've done your homework and identified the right person for the job of Senator or Representative, spread the word. Get involved in ousting incumbents of both parties who stand in the way of progress.

I realize there is a lot going on and we only have so much time for politics. Accordingly, here are some of the key issues to follow in the months ahead. First up, will we get a real budget or will the obstructionist Dems in the resistance movement hold us hostage again with another threatened government shutdown? We can count on President Trump not to be blackmailed in this fashion but can you count on your Republican Senators and Representatives too or will they be bullied into harmful concessions? DACA is no reason to cave. The President has offered a generous compromise that the Democrats could certainly sell to their voters. Do they really want to help the so called Dreamers or do they just want to make political hay? If anyone in the GOP ranks calls for a skinny bill that gives in on a pathway to citizenship for a wall only, mark them down for ouster. The only way to achieve border security is the wall plus an end to the visa lottery and chain migration. Remember what the President said, "Americans are Dreamers too."

Will we be able to move on to infrastructure or will the Dems poison the well on the DACA/budget showdown? If the President somehow pulls off the impossible, then infrastructure should be a piece of cake, right? One would think so since the Dems love to spend money. But I encourage caution here. We've seen this movie before. President Obama spent at least $800 billion on "infrastructure" during his time in office. Then why are we facing crumbling roads, bridges, highways, ports and airports? Don't you remember when he had to admit that his vaunted shovel-ready projects weren't really shovel-ready? What happened to all of that money then? The simple fact of the matter folks is that most of it was wasted. A lot of it was used to add new layers of fat onto our already bloated government bureaucracy. The moral of the story is that rebuilding our infrastructure is not as easy as it might seem even with bi-partisan support.

Watch out for more wasteful spending. Yes, there are a lot of big spenders among the Republicans too. Waste is a bi-partisan problem. It's enough to make Deplorables hope for successful obstructionism when it comes to infrastructure … but I jest … I think. Our best hope is that we have a Businessman-in-Chief and a fabulously successful, experienced builder in the White House. If anyone can reign in big government to pull this off, it's Donald Trump. Look for him to have heavy involvement. He will target the right projects and then push for completion ahead of schedule and under budget. Most importantly, he will seek participation from the private sector to avoid typical government waste and mismanagement.

There is a lot of craziness and danger in the world. It's hard to keep track of everything. For the purpose of this exercise, let's focus on five hot spots. Don't be lulled into a false sense of security regarding radical Islamic terrorism and stand firm against the Palestinian Authority and Pakistan unless they show a willingness to cooperate and seek true peace. Will the Congress back the President in holding Iran's feet to the fire? We need to insist upon significant changes to put some teeth into the Iran Nuclear Deal or let it lapse. We need to continue to use a carrot and stick approach with China and Russia. Diplomacy is important but we can never forget that they are our adversaries. We should seek out opportunities to serve our mutual interests but stand ready with economic pressure and military might if needed. As for North Korea, the clock is running down fast. We can no longer kick the can down the road. This is truly an existential threat and if anyone, Democrat or Republican, tries to play politics in this area, we cannot budge. We must intervene militarily if it's the only way to prevent North Korea from gaining the capability to deliver nuclear war heads to our shores. Being prepared to back up this threat is the only hope for a diplomatic solution.

The last trend to follow is perhaps the most important. The ongoing investigations are going to get very ugly. We will need a step ladder to stand above the lies, corruption and cover-ups. Misery loves company so, as a last resort, the Dems and bad actors in the Deep State will resort to moral relativism. They will claim that the Trump campaign was just as guilty as the Obama Camp who tried to determine the outcome of the 2016 election and then undermine the Trump presidency by using the power of the FBI, DOJ and State Department to play politics. This is no place to compromise!

The media will remain complicit in this cover-up. They must be held accountable. Don't rely heavily on CNN, MSNBC, CBS, ABC, NBC and other such slanted sources for your news. At least take a peek at FNC and other conservative outlets to get both sides of the story. Put on your thinking caps people! Don't be distracted by shiny objects. If Dems and the media try to tell you they're concerned about national security, don't buy it. When have they ever cared about national security? They certainly didn't raise any issues when top secret information was leaked out over and over again to try to discredit President Trump. They turned a blind eye to all of the classified national secrets that Hillary Clinton exposed to our enemies over her unsecured, private server. Bottom line, don't rely on rhetoric. Demand to see the evidence behind claims from both sides and make up your own minds!

Beware of any RINOs who attempt to maintain the status quo by appearing to be forgiving while letting transgressors off with a slap on the wrist.

Demand that justice be served as it would be if you or I had committed a fraction of the crimes involved. We must draw a line in the sand! I'm not being dramatic when I say that the fate of our Republic rests on whether this corruption is rooted out, exposed to the light of day and eradicated with swift, sure justice. Anyone who committed the treasonous acts of trying to surreptitiously determine the outcome of a presidential election or undermine the new government of our duly elected President should be put in jail. There should be no leniency or clemency because of wealth or political standing. This includes the folks at Fusion GPS, Peter Strzok, Lisa Page, James Comey, Andrew McCabe, Rod Rosenstein, Andrew Weissmann, Bruce Ohr, Nellie Ohr, Christopher Steele, Robert Mueller, Loretta Lynch, Bill Clinton, Hillary Clinton and Barack Obama.

There you have it my Deplorable friends. Our mission is clear. We're at the start of a new renaissance much like the one President Reagan ushered in forty years ago. Like then as now, it's not a top-down movement. Although President Trump's leadership is crucial, this reformation is being driven by you and me; the American people. Like in the aftermath of Jimmy Carter and years of sliding to the Left, we're at a crossroads again. Only this time we're much further Left and precipitously close to an extremely dangerous cliff. We face ominous threats at home and around the globe. But still our future is bright. We can see it just over the horizon. This is no time to rest or be complacent as President Trump said but rather to keep marching forward to claim our best days ahead. Please go to the polls this year in droves with this one glorious thought in mind. Let's make America great again. We can do it!

Acknowledgments:

Thankfully, I don't need to burden you with a comprehensive bibliography or long list of footnotes. That's because I took a simple approach to chronicling the past year in politics. I paid attention to the news and took good notes. I'm not going to name every news source I followed but can tell you I took advantage of a wide variety of outlets. As much as I may have wanted to at times, I couldn't avoid the mainstream media. It served as the best window into the lunacy of the so called Resistance. Although I wasn't a regular consumer of liberal sources like CNN, MSNBC, Huff Post, ABC, NBC and CBS, I caught their headlines regularly through other outlets and social media feeds. I must sheepishly admit I couldn't figure out how to turn off my Yahoo News feed on my phone ... LOL!

I can't honestly credit any particular sources but will offer thanks to some of my favorite outlets. As for daily news, fair and balanced FNC ranks at the top for me. As noted earlier herein, I don't have a lot of respect for certain programs, hosts and guests of theirs but all-in-all, their coverage deserves praise. My greatest source of information came from the internet so I guess I should thank who, Al Gore? Seriously though, it's a wonderful technical innovation that has done a lot of harm (Facebook and Google come to mind) but more so has empowered Deplorable people in an incredible way.

Lastly, I have to offer kudos to some of the local outlets here in St. Louis. We seem to be blessed with more than our share of talented truth-tellers. Local news talk station FM 97.1 has a fantastic line-up including some noteworthy nationally syndicated folks. Among their locals, Jamie Allman and Marc Cox are outstanding. The most entertaining and boldest purveyor of the truth in the Lou is Kevin Slaten on AM 1190. He's known as the King of Sports Talk in our town but also spices things up with his in-depth, no-holds-barred political analysis.

Final Words in Parting:

I followed my own advice and continued to stay on top of things, particularly in regard to the critical topics listed in Part Four: Unfinished Business, as I prepared this *Deplorable 2018 Election Guide* for publication. Amazing developments occurred in these short few weeks and I had to at least mention them before closing.

Head of the Snake: They released more Strzok/Page texts from the ones supposedly lost. Not surprisingly, many echoed more hatred for Deplorables, in particular Pro-Life Marchers. But stunningly, they revealed that President Obama was personally involved in keeping track of their nefarious deeds. A strange email from renowned Benghazi liar Susan Rice to herself appeared to reveal an attempt to rewrite history and cover up President Obama's deep involvement in the efforts to undermine the Trump presidency. She wrote to herself that in a meeting two weeks prior, shortly before leaving office, President Obama had told top Justice and FBI officials to do things "by the book" ... very strange indeed.

Ransom Payment: The Dems and Republicans reached a bi-partisan budget deal without DACA. It thankfully secured much needed funding for the military but, unfortunately, added a like amount for more domestic largesse. In true swamp-like fashion, big spenders from both parties combined efforts to add another $400 billion to our already crippling deficit. This gave Deplorables all the more reason to bounce people from both parties in the 2018 mid-terms. We need more true conservatives and fiscal hawks!

Korean Mata Hari: Murderous North Korean tyrant, Kim Jong-un sent his younger, better looking sister, Kim Yo Jong, to the Olympics for a charm offensive. The insane liberal media took the bait hook, line and sinker and hailed the poisonous propaganda princess as somehow lovely and heroic compared to Donald Trump and Mike Pence. The media blatantly sided with evil over good.

Portrait of Evil: Evil over good reared its ugly head again in brazen fashion when the media fawned over newly released, freakish portraits of President Obama and First Lady Michelle. No one seemed to mind that the former President chose Kihinde Wiley to paint their likenesses. Wiley had made a name for himself by painting portraits of black women holding the severed heads of white women. This was just another addition to the basket of truly deplorable friends of the ex-President such as racist, America-hating Reverend Jeremiah Wright and domestic terrorist William Ayers.

"Tolerant" Intolerance: Evil continued to ooze out into the open, this time on *The View* where Joy Behar mocked Vice President Mike Pence for his Christian faith. A guest of the show, disgruntled former White House aide Omorosa, described the VP as an "extreme" Christian who believed Jesus talked to him. Behar chimed in and pronounced the Vice President to be mentally ill. Deplorables took this personally because many of us knew the truth that Jesus talked to us daily through His word, the Holy Bible. Deplorables resented the fact that "tolerant" liberals felt Christians were fair game for such intolerance and persecution. Joy Behar didn't criticize Oprah when she said she hadn't heard a call from Jesus to run for president.

Self-Protection: Another horrific high school massacre occurred in Parkland, Florida. Before the seventeen bodies could be laid to rest, the Dems started clamoring about gun control. Why didn't they call for gun control when police officers were gunned down indiscriminately? The shooter was under treatment for mental health issues when he purchased the gun. His adoptive parents allowed him to have the gun knowing full well that he suffered from mental problems. They put his gun in a locked safe but gave him a key!

Many of the surviving students said they knew the shooter was a problem waiting to happen. One man had contacted the FBI when the shooter posted his murderous intentions online but the FBI failed to follow through on the lead that would have surely prevented the rampage. The FBI was too busy running down Russian collusion hoaxes, committing adultery with fellow agents and sending thousands of personal texts. The Broward County Sheriff's Office received forty-five complaints about Nikolas Cruz but sat on their hands.

Liberals blamed guns and the NRA. No one said a peep about the real culprits of mass killings: the perpetrators. Of course, there was no mention of the other tools of mass destruction used such as fertilizer bombs, knives, crockpot bombs, cars and trucks. Taking guns away from law-abiding citizens would magically stop law breakers. Increasing the age of gun ownership from eighteen to twenty-one would do the trick. Wait, most of the preceding evil sickos and mass murderers were over eighteen. Eliminating bump stocks would make everyone feel better but would it have stopped Nikolas Cruz? Deplorables learned one thing from Parkland, Florida: we had to protect ourselves rather than relying on the government.

Russian (Window) Dressing: Special Counsel Robert Mueller issued thirteen indictments against Russian nationals who meddled in our 2016 election. The liberal medial had a field day in somehow claiming this showed the Trump campaign had colluded with them. They completely ignored Deputy AG Rod Rosenstein's clear, public statement that, although the Russians meddled, they hadn't affected the outcome of the election and NO AMERICANS had wittingly worked with the Russian malefactors. This news actually helped to vindicate President Trump once again but the media turned it around to somehow indict him in the court of public opinion. The liberal media were so blinded by hatred and TDS that they couldn't even tell the difference between meddling and collusion. This was window dressing designed to justify the millions of dollars wasted on the Russian collusion hoax.

Liberals Gone Wild: Rep. Joaquin Castro (D, TX) compared Russian meddling in the 2016 election to Al Qaeda's 9/11 attacks on the World Trade Center where almost three-thousand Americans were killed. Rep. Jerry Nadler (D, NY) compared Russian meddling to the Japanese attack at Pearl Harbor where over four-thousand Americans were killed or wounded and it prompted America's involvement in WWII. This was more liberal insanity.

Where in the hell were these people in 2014-2016 when Obama presided over the Russian meddling??? Then President Obama had mocked candidate Mitt Romney for declaring Russia to be America's greatest geopolitical threat. Candidate Obama thought it was cute to say that the 1980s called and wanted their foreign policy back.

During the 2016 campaign, President Obama chided candidate Trump and declared confidently that no one could disrupt our democratic elections. He admonished Donald Trump to stop making excuses and get back to campaigning. President Obama made these remarks knowing full well that the Russians were trying to disrupt our election process. Donald Trump took his advice and campaigned in Pennsylvania, Wisconsin, Michigan and elsewhere and pulled off the greatest upset in American political history.

Investigate the Investigator: The judge assigned to the Mueller indictments had to recuse himself because of his involvement in the FISA request. The new judge assigned to the case against Michael Flynn ordered all exculpatory evidence to be turned over to him. This meant he wanted to see evidence in Mueller's possession that would tend to exonerate Flynn. What ... did this mean the judge questioned whether Flynn actually lied to the FBI??? Did Mueller coerce Flynn into copping a plea by threatening him with financial ruin? Something smelled rotten in D. C. Perhaps this judge was about to blow the lid off the corrupt Mueller investigation. PAY CLOSE ATTENTION TO DEVELOPMENTS ON THIS ONE FOLKS!

President Trump is All Ears: The most transparent President in our history gave Americans another unprecedented look into his governance by holding a televised "listening session" at the White House with survivors of school shootings in Columbine, Sandy Hook and Parkland. All sides were afforded the opportunity to express their views while President Trump remained open to all suggestions. I couldn't help but cringe when one distraught, liberal student emotionally asked repeatedly why he, at eighteen, could still purchase a "weapon of war." To my frustration, no one had the guts or knowledge to tell the young man that no nation on earth would arm it's military with AR-15 semi-automatic rifles.

Teachers in the group objected to the obvious solution of arming them or administrators … true insanity in the wake of Parkland. Deplorables thought about Nancy Pelosi's recent admission that she hoped common sense restrictions would provide a slippery slope toward an end to the Second Amendment. I didn't worry too much though since I realized any sensible legislation would be shot down by the Dems. They might unfortunately allow more kids to be slaughtered rather than giving any legislative victory to President Trump.

One thing really bothered me though. When would there be protests, vigils and listening sessions for the surviving spouses and children of all the police officers gunned down on a regular basis? When would there be such public sympathy shown for victims in the murder capital of America: Chicago? That didn't fit the narrative since Chicago boasted some of the toughest gun laws in the country.

As details found their way to the Press, we learned that the Broward County Sheriff's Office had prohibited first responders from entering the school to provide emergency care to the shooting victims. Perhaps they could have saved some lives. We also found out that at least one and perhaps four armed members of the Broward County Sheriff's Office cowered outside Stoneman High School while Nikolas Cruz gunned down seventeen people. There could have been an armed intervention that would have saved many lives but these cowards wilted in the face of danger or were ordered to stand down. Sheriff Scott Israel of Broward County denounced one of the four people who failed to do their duty but refused to take any responsibility himself. He said he had provided "amazing" leadership. Just days before, he had attended a staged CNN forum and blamed the NRA even though he knew at the time that his office had failed.

Political Knuckle-headedness: Purdue University issued official speech guidelines recommending that people stop using the term "man." And so it went ... liberalism remained a mental illness folks.

Power Grab: The Founders did their best to thwart government tyranny by establishing a balance of power between the executive, legislative and judicial branches of our Republic. Since liberals had long detested the Constitution, they had followed a careful strategy to undermine the will of the people by tipping the scales toward unelected judges. This resulted in one, small hotbed of activist judges, the wacky Ninth Circuit in San Francisco, having control over the Executive Branch, Congress and the American people.

President Obama had admitted on numerous occasions that his executive order on DACA was unconstitutional. President Trump had tried to undo the damage with an executive order of his own ending

DACA. The Ninth Circuit, which never objected to Obama's order, stepped in and declared President Trump's order unconstitutional. Having seen this maneuver many times already on his travel ban and other measures, the President tried to expedite things by taking his case directly to the Supreme Court. They declined to hear the case and sent it back to the Ninth Circuit.

This may have been the proper ruling from a legal standpoint but it was completely unfair and wholly inconsistent. How could one President's executive order establishing DACA be constitutional but another ending it be unconstitutional? President Trump had tried to do the right thing by forcing Congress to do their job. In the process, he had been more than charitable by allowing DACA to stand for six months in the interim. Then he went further by offering amnesty to 1.8 million illegal "Dreamers" in exchange for border security and a lasting solution to our immigration problem.

The Democrats screwed the "Dreamers" and rejected his generous offer to deny the President a bi-partisan win. Then they had their lackeys in the Ninth Circuit do their dirty work to thwart the President and undermine the will of the American people in order to, in their minds, gain political leverage heading into the 2018 mid-terms. Don't let it happen, Deplorables! Hold them accountable and give the President a larger majority in the House and sixty-vote margin in the

Senate so we can continue to make America great again!

America's Godly Heritage: Only FNC gave full coverage to the events leading up to and including the burial of Rev. Billy Graham, America's Pastor. Why didn't the mainstream media go beyond barely a mention in passing of God's humble servant? It came down to this: a battle between good and evil. I'll let you discern which is which.

Days before the burial in North Carolina, President Trump, First Lady Melania and a host of other dignitaries gathered with the Graham family in the Capitol Rotunda to honor the life of Rev. Billy Graham in his service to our Lord and Savior, Jesus Christ. This poignant ceremony pointed the only way to truly make America great again. That is, for America to be great we need to be good … and the only way to be good again is to turn back to God and welcome Jesus back into our schools, businesses, halls of government, the public square and our homes as one nation under God.

<u>Other Books by Steve Stranghoener:</u>

Uncle Sam's White Hat

Deadly Preference

530 Reasons Why Deplorables Won

Veeper

Ferguson Miracle

God-Whacked!

Cha-Cha Chandler: Teen Demonologist

Straight Talk about Christian Misconceptions

The Last Prophet: Doomsday Diary

The Last Prophet: Imminent End

Murder by Chance: Blood Moon Lunacy of Lew Carew

Asunder: The Tale of the Renaissance Killer

Tracts in Time

All of these titles are available under Books/Steve Stranghoener at <u>www.amazon.com</u>.

Made in the USA
Columbia, SC
17 August 2018